Company of Angels

Four Plays by John Retallack

HANNAH AND HANNA

CLUB ASYLUM

VIRGINS

RISK

OBERON BOOKS
LONDON

First published in 2007 by Oberon Books Ltd.
521 Caledonian Road, London N7 9RH
Tel: 020 7607 3637 / Fax: 020 7607 3629
info@oberonbooks.com
www.oberonbooks.com

with the exception of *Hannah and Hanna* first published in
The Drama Book (English and Media Centre, 2002)

A catalogue record for this book is available from the British Library.

ISBN: 1 84002 725 8 / 978-1-84002-725-9

Cover photograph by Kevin Low

Printed in Great Britain by Antony Rowe Ltd, Chippenham.

Contents

Preface

This quartet of plays is partially the result of a love affair with European theatre. Its influence on his work is obvious but, in his desire to break with convention, John Retallack has set shiny new 'gold standards' of his own for anyone involved in creating work for and about teenagers.

Common to each of the works in this brand new anthology are big and often uncomfortable ideas, and an über-intention to get to the crux of matter we'd much rather avoid. In *Virgins* we're invited to consider the folly of sensationalising sexual awakening. Following a night on a bender Jack finds it impossible to recall recent events and convinces himself he's had casual sex. He rapidly slides into a state of anxiety and self-loathing, convinced he's picked up a sexually transmitted infection. This tortuous scenario could be alleviated if his family were less British and more Northern European about the situation. Crisis point has got to be reached before gentle and constructive talk can begin.

Club Asylum and *Hannah and Hanna* are a duo. These two are about the thorny issue of immigration and I encourage you to read them side by side. This way you'll discover what is becoming a hallmark of John and his Company of Angel's work. Both the content of the work and the avant-garde way it is brought to us reflect the company's optimism about teenagers' capacity to embrace new ideas. The two protagonists in *Hannah and Hanna* are the same age, share the same name and live in Margate. That's where their similarities might end because their life experiences so far are vastly different. They can keep fanning the flames of their elders' fears and resentments or they can choose to become friends.

Like *Virgins*, *Hannah and Hanna* follows a linear narrative. In *Club Asylum* John experiments more boldly with dance, movement and ensemble, and although this is sequentially the second play of the canon (*Virgins* happened later) it paved the way for *Risk*, the last part of the quartet. *Risk* is by far the most forensic examination of teenage life. It's chilling to learn that much of the content is based on conversations with teenagers in Glasgow. But this isn't verbatim theatre. It's a muscular work of great poetic sophistication. As I write, it is in rehearsal and I simply can't wait to see it.

Suzy Graham-Adriani
Connections Producer, National Theatre

Introduction

During the period that I was artistic director of Oxford Stage Company (1989–1999) I won an Arts Council bursary to go and see professional theatre for children and young people in France, Holland, Italy and Germany. I saw great work in each of these countries but Holland opened up a new world for me.

I went to a small festival in the south of the country that specialised in this area, the 'Kunst Junior' Festival in Den Bosch. The work there was inspirational. Content was contemporary with a clear political awareness; the acting companies were strong and well-versed in ensemble technique and spirit; viewed simply as theatre it was ravishing – yet shows took place in school gymnasiums in daylight. The work was strikingly sophisticated and assertively modern in delivery because it had a clear purpose – to intrigue and to entertain young audiences who would soon be citizens with a vote to cast and role to play in the world. These performances surpassed the drab surroundings in which they were placed and gained an almost transcendental theatrical power in doing so.

At the time of one performance, Wederzijds' production of *Hitler's Childhood*, I wrote in my diary:

> Adults know much about the end of Hitler, but who knows about the beginning? Is a fascist dictator born evil or is he made evil? These are pertinent questions in a part of Belgium where the Vlaams Blok [the Flemish Far Right Wing] is winning so many votes. This performance was accurately judged and conceived with great imagination and intelligence. It was also very beautiful to look at and to listen to. It was the most original work I've seen all year. It makes theatre for young people a fresh prospect and makes me speculate if it might be an exciting step to take personally.

Wederzijds were – and are still – one of the leading companies that produce new work for children. Oxford Stage Company and Wederzijds worked together frequently between 1993 and 1998, and the relationship with its artistic leader, Ad de Bont, continues today through Company of Angels.

In Ad de Bont's work I found a depth of thought and a stylistic flair that I was familiar with from growing up and competing in a theatre world whose standards in England were set – for me – by Mike Alfreds' Shared Experience, Theatre de Complicite, Cheek by Jowl, Deborah Warner's Kick Theatre Company and in France and Germany by Ariane Mnouchkine, Peter Brook and Peter Stein. These were my lasting formative influences. ATC (1978–85) and Oxford Stage Company were shaped by watching the work of these companies and through meeting and knowing the directors in question. They were my 'gold standard'.

But none of these great directors and companies made work for children. If the books I read to my children were so good, written and published in England, why were they not matched by a similar achievement in the performing arts? Why was funding so low and why was there such limited respect for this genre of theatre work? All the brilliant companies that I mention above played overseas and were known in Europe – but an English company at a young people's theatre festival in Europe was a rare sight.

My surprise in discovering the work of Wederzijds (and several similar groups in Holland) was that these companies were clearly working to their own 'gold standard'. It was, for me, like finding an undiscovered theatre world as exacting and inspiring as the one that shaped me. I am a trained teacher and an untrained theatre director. The discovery of work of such originality and engagement in the domain of theatre for young people linked worlds that I thought had no connection.

Later I was to learn that Holland had a real theatre revolution in the late '60s when students pelted mainstream theatre productions with tomatoes because they deemed that it was no longer relevant to the times. In the early '70s, many talented young writers, actors and directors formed ensembles and invented a new type of theatre that was performed outside theatre buildings and centred on audiences of children and teenagers. It has grown since then into a fully funded network of independent companies throughout the Netherlands.

From 1996 to 2000, with the poet Maura Dooley, I ran an annual series of ten-day writers' workshops for Performing Arts Labs at a retreat in deepest Kent. Although I was there as a tutor/director I actually felt that I learnt rather more than I taught. The tutors on the courses were themselves well-known writers from England or Holland – Bryony Lavery, April de Angelis, Suzanne van Lohuizen, Pauline Mol – and the participating writers (ten per retreat) themselves were of a high calibre. About fifty new plays emerged from the PAL retreats – but the play I wanted someone to write remained unwritten.

I wanted a contemporary political play about young people. It has long seemed to me that it is young people who experience social change in the most direct and brutal way. Put very simply indeed, I think that teenagers live outdoors and adults live indoors. If there's a riot or a flood or a fight, or if it's the middle of the night, it's not usually the kids at home worrying about mum and dad, it's the other way about. So I wanted to put teenagers centre stage in a story about the grown-up world.

In 2000 I wrote *Hannah and Hanna*, a play about two young women, one British, the other a Kosovan asylum seeker, living in Margate. The Channel Theatre Company co-produced the play. We rehearsed it in Margate in the early summer of 2001 and then took it to the Edinburgh Festival for a month. The performance that I will always remember was the first night at Margate Theatre Royal; the tiny show on the big stage of one of the country's oldest theatres with most of the local police force in the stalls (they formed the backbone of the amateur dramatic society at that time) and a range of asylum seekers and refugees from all over the area in the dress circle. Disruptive elements kept their distance outside the theatre and the show briefly united the house in warm and sustained applause.

Jan Ryan of UK Arts International toured *Hannah and Hanna* several times both in Britain and overseas with the British Council. The success of the play allowed me to form what I had been planning since I left Oxford Stage Company – a company that would promote new and experimental work for young audiences: Company of Angels.

* * *

Movement and dance form an important part of *Hannah and Hanna* and it was through working with choreographer Andy Howitt that we came up with the idea for *Club Asylum*.

Andy runs Y DANCE (formerly Scottish Youth Dance), and his company have revolutionised the relationship between young people and dance in Scotland. His company's first very popular CD-ROM for schools is called *ABCD* ('Any Body Can Dance'). He is an inspiration to many, myself included.

Andy and I both liked and admired the work of the Belgian companies Victoria (theatre) and Rosas (dance). We also sought a dramatic theatre form that addressed cultural and political issues without having to obey the rules of the well-made play. We wanted to excite kids who had never seen theatre before and also seasoned theatregoers; we wanted the show to work in a conventional theatre and in a school dining hall at ten in the morning. We sought urgency, excitement, movement in the minds of a young audience – and the prospect of debate, either with the performers or later in the school between teachers and pupils when the company had moved on.

Club Asylum addresses the same theme as *Hannah and Hanna* but in a different form. Its foundation is in dance and it has a more poetic and choric use of text than its predecessor.

Club Asylum toured throughout Scotland and played in many areas where asylum seekers were just a rumour. The form of *Club Asylum* – and of *Risk* too – allows a company to cover a very wide spectrum of opinion and experience in a very concentrated form. The juxtaposition of text and dance allows the explosive nature of certain themes to gain very powerful expression. The body is eloquent to all young people.

Unlike the other three plays in this volume, *Virgins* is an 'indoor' play – no one can actually get way from home. Even when they're outdoors, the characters talk and think about each other. *Virgins* is built around dance. This is because there is so much that the family cannot actually say to each other; the parents, in particular, cannot find the words to talk about sexuality and the intense emotions that it generates either with each other or with their children. Hence this is a play in which dialogue comes in two forms – spoken and unspoken text. Or, to put it another way, what the family can say to each other and what they can't. With the dance – the unspoken text – a company is free to choose its own music and its own choreography. Nothing is set.

When *Virgins* was on tour I was often asked about the experience of being a writer-director. In my case, I've been a director longer than I've been a writer and I tend to stage the narrative plays (*Hannah and Hanna* and *Virgins*) in my mind when I write them. The opposite is the case with *Club Asylum* and *Risk*; with these texts I try to make the words as kinaesthetic as possible but leave the staging completely open for the company that performs the piece. They can be staged in any number of ways. The main thing about being a writer-director is that by the time rehearsals begin you have to know what you want but be open about the way that you will get there. 'What you want' never looks quite how you expected it to look.

The shorter introductions which precede each play give a fuller picture of their individual aims, how each of them came about and the specific context in which they were made. To me, though, whatever else it may be, the challenge of creating great work for young people is always an aesthetic one – experiment and innovation are constantly required.

Andy Howitt and I collaborated on *Hannah and Hanna*, *Club Asylum*, *I'm A Young Boy Just Like You* (a short film made with young Albanian refugees) and now *Risk*, the final play in this volume. *Risk*, like *Club Asylum*, is inspired by Glasgow. The workshop and research happened there and all the actors are from the city. It came about because a lot of teenagers have to face very adult decisions early in life. And this happens often because the adults to whom they are closest are immature and want to go on living like teenagers. Being a 'teenager' was often seen as being a predictable set of experiences that happened to everyone in roughly the same order. Nothing could be further from the truth. Adolescence for many is a state of chaos; the stories in *Risk* are about individuals who have to face big choices, big risks.

About Company of Angels

Company of Angels was founded on the following beliefs:

1 The political and emotional centre of social change frequently revolves around children and young people.

2 Theatre has a counter-cultural identity when it is prepared to leave its familiar audiences and buildings behind.

3 Theatre to young 'non-theatre' audiences in 'non-theatre' spaces can stimulate avant-garde work of originality and beauty.

It was named Company of Angels not only because it would have to multiply on a wing and a prayer, but because I thought that Angels could turn up anywhere at any time – a hospital ward or a village hall or a school classroom, for example.

Its stated mission is to broaden the definition of theatre for young people through experimental projects and new productions of a high artistic standard.

The company found an excellent range of partners from the beginning (Channel Theatre Company, the Tron Theatre, macrobert, the Arcola Theatre, Polka Theatre, Quicksilver, Caird Company), as well as a number of established European playwrights whose work had not been seen in Britain before (for example, Helene Verburgh, Joël Jouannaeu, Marco Baliani, Ad de Bont, Henning Mankell and Lot Vekemaans). David Farr's *Crime and Punishment in Dalston* produced at the Arcola in East London in 2002 was also a big hit for the company.

The ingenious ways in which we chose to 'umbrella' new work from Europe helped greatly; *Young Europe* and *Theatre Café* excited attention as theatrical events. *Theatre Café* is a kind of bohemian space for plays, part-chamber, part-catwalk, in which – as one critic put it – 'extreme readings' took place, script-in-hand. It presented 12 European premieres over as many days to young people and to theatre people on the lookout for new work to bring into their repertoire. All the writers visited *Theatre Café* in person and participated in forums and discussions. In 2007, with a generous Culture 2000 grant from the European Commission, the project happened in four different countries: Holland, France, Estonia and England.

A new company has to work overtime to survive. We did so by stringing together a host of project grants from Trusts and Foundations that just about sustained sufficient monthly income to keep a functioning office. The real breakthrough came when Teresa Ariosto joined as Producer in January 2002. Teresa had worked for the Italian Theatre Institute in Rome and for the Blickfelder International Theatre Festival For Young Audiences in Zurich. She knew the repertoire of plays extremely well and she spoke the languages in which the plays were written. Five years on, Teresa has greatly expanded the network of partners with whom the company works and she steered the company towards its status as an Arts Council revenue client since April 2004.

The funding that we receive is essential to us and it has allowed us to expand to a staff of four and to develop projects like *Young Angels*. The aim of this programme is to impress upon theatre-makers and the industry in general that new work for young audiences is an exciting arena for artistic innovation and experiment. As well as raising funds for this, it is the company's intention to open its own studio/laboratory in 2008/9. The purpose of this will be to make the first space for professional theatre-makers to experiment with new performance work for children and teenagers.

We continue to work with a wide range of partners; it would be impossible to fund the work we do on our own. In a way, the necessity of finding partners has been the best thing that happened to Company of Angels. Instead of becoming a small company enclosed within its own aesthetic and culture, we have had no option but to win others round to what we do. It has widened the Company's network greatly and, most important of all, opened us to fresh ways of thinking about what we do.

John Retallack, 2007

Timeline

2001 • Company of Angels founded.
 • (June) *Hannah and Hanna* opens at the Theatre Royal Margate, co-produced with Channel Theatre Company.
 • (August) *Hannah and Hanna* wins a Herald Angel Award at the Edinburgh Fringe Festival.
 • (September) *Hannah and Hanna* runs at the Arcola Theatre, London.

2002 • (January) Teresa Ariosto joins the company as Producer.
 • *Club Asylum* produced in collaboration with macrobert Arts Centre, Stirling.
 • Production of David Farr's *Crime and Punishment in Dalston* at the Arcola Theatre, London.
 • *Fathers and Eggs* by Heleen Verburg and *The Wild Girl* by John Retallack,

two 'classroom plays' for children, tour London primary schools in a co-production with Quicksilver Theatre.

- (February) *Hannah and Hanna* presented at the Time Out Critics' Choice Festival at BAC, London, and produced by UK Arts International on its first national tour.

2003 • *Gap Theatre Project*, a unique peer-mentoring initiative involving gap-year students and Year 6 primary school children, piloted at an inner London primary school.

- *Asylum Seeker Narratives*, a community project of drama, dance and video workshops involving young Albanian asylum seekers, takes place in conjunction with Albanian Youth Action.

- *Hannah and Hanna* tours to India with the support of the British Council; UK Arts International's second national tour of the play nominated for a TMA Award and a Race in the Media Award.

2004 • *Young Europe*, a mini-festival of three new European plays from France (*Kadouma's Island* by Joël Jouanneau), Italy (*Little Angels* by Marco Baliani) and the UK (*Sweetpeter* by John Retallack), co-produced with Polka Theatre and tours the South East.

- *Theatre Café*, a series of 'site-specific' rehearsed readings presenting new European plays to UK audiences, is launched at the Arcola Theatre in collaboration with the Caird Company.

- *I Am A Young Boy Just Like You*, the film resulting from the *Asylum Seeker Narratives* scheme, is screened at the EUnet Arts conference in Cork.

- UK Arts International produces *Hannah and Hanna* for a third national tour. The show also tours to Malaysia supported by the British Council

2005 • Second *Gap Theatre Project* run in association with Yerbury Primary School.

- *Project R*, the successor to *Asylum Seeker Narratives*, started in collaboration with ATTIC Theatre Company.

- *I Am A Young Boy Just Like You* screened at the Discovery Festival in Stirling and at the Medical Foundation in London.

- *Hannah and Hanna* plays at the Greenwich Theatre in London and tours to the Philippines supported by the British Council.

2006 • (May) First *Young Directors Programme* in association with Drama Centre London, providing an opportunity for young theatre-makers to create and test new work for young audiences.

- (August) *Virgins* co-produced with The Junction, Cambridge, at the Edinburgh Fringe Festival and on a national tour, including performance at the Lockpicker's Ball new writing festival in Liverpool.

- The company starts its search for Angels Studio, a space for professional theatre-makers to experiment with new performance work for children and teenagers.

2007 • (February) *Risk* opens at the Tron Theatre, Glasgow, followed by a national tour.
   • *Truckstop* by award-winning Dutch writer Lot Vekemans co-produced with Eastern Angles Theatre Company, touring nationally in the autumn.
   • The European edition of *Theatre Café* presents ten plays from ten different countries in four events across Europe, in collaboration with hetMUZTheater, Amsterdam, Le Grand Bleu, Lille and VAT Teater, Tallinn.
   • *Young Angels Directors, Designers & Writers* expands the idea of the 2006 *Young Directors Programme* in association with Drama Centre and Soho Theatre, bringing together young creative professionals to collaborate on new work for young audiences.
   • *Gap Theatre Project* extended to the Cambridge area.

2008 • *Young Angels Theatre-Makers*, a new bursary scheme to attract young artists to the field of theatre for young audiences, piloted at The Junction, Cambridge, as preparation for a national *Young Angels* scheme in association with the Junction, the Royal Exchange Theatre, Manchester, and the Hampstead Theatre, London.

Company Details

Director John Retallack
Producer Teresa Ariosto
Administrator Vanessa Fagan
Project Co-ordinator Jennifer Lewin
Finance Manager David Harris
Board Rob West (Chair), Cathy Bereznicki, Penny Black, Jennifer Jones, Philippe Le Moine, Jeremy Smeeth, Denise Wong

Contact www.companyofangels.co.uk
126 Cornwall Road, London, SE1 8TQ
020 7928 2811
info@companyofangels.co.uk

HANNAH AND HANNA

for Judith and Alina Hibberd

Background

I wrote *Hannah and Hanna* after running a few workshops for teenagers in and around Margate.

At the time I wrote the play, teenagers in schools in Britain were told very little about why large groups of people from other countries arrived overnight. All they knew is that they were 'asylums', people from nowhere. National and local community leaders showed little interest in 'introducing' these strangers to the local community. In school classrooms, pupils sometimes did not know where the boy or girl at the next desk was actually from. That's hard for those who turn up here and hard on the local people who don't know why they're at the bus stop, in the waiting room at the dentist's or slowing up the queue at the supermarket check-out. In small towns, the reaction to asylum seekers could be more violent, not less. In Margate, in 2000, there was an overnight dumping of hundreds of Kosovans. The town could talk of little else; pensioners were outraged, teenagers declared war, the local newspapers had a story that would run and run.

How could a local Margate teenager – in that climate – ever meet, let alone befriend, a Kosovan teenager who'd survived the invasion of her country and ended up in Margate? And at what point, supposing that a friendship did develop, would the two girls open up to each other? Were there any circumstances that could bring about a real and unprompted exchange between them?

I wanted to acknowledge the role of us, the British audience, in the drama of the refugee. 'We' are the hosts who determine the fate of such people, our guests. 'We' are central characters, not onlookers and outsiders. To the asylum seekers, 'we' are the main players. That's why I started with two teenagers; they mimic the attitudes of their parents, yet, unlike their parents, they still have time to change their minds.

Hannah and Hanna is a strong narrative and it has struck a nerve in many places. It is playing now in France, Germany, Holland and Portugal and it has been seen in several countries beyond Europe.

Hannah and Hanna is often performed in schools; once I saw twelve Hanna/hs do a 'relay' performance of the play.

It can be performed with almost no props or set whatsoever (this happened twice on tour when the set failed to arrive).

When the play is translated or performed by schools, different locations for the story and different songs are sometimes chosen.

Characters

HANNAH, English, 16

HANNA (Xhevahinja), ethnic Albanian asylum seeker from Kosovo,16

The play is set in Margate and Kosovo between summer 1999 and spring 2000.

Hannah and Hanna was first performed at the Channel Theatre Company Studio on 21 June 2001 with the following company:

HANNAH, Alyson Coote
HANNA, Celia Meiras

Director John Retallack
Designer Phil Newman
Musical Arranger Karl James
Movement Andy Howitt
Lighting Guy Retallack / Nicci Spalding

Hannah and Hanna was made possible by a 'Making Art Matter' award from South East Arts and further grants from the Esmée Fairbairn Foundation, Lloyds TSB and Awards For All. The play was a co-production with Channel Theatre Company in Margate.

The play won a Glasgow Herald Angel at the Edinburgh Fringe, was part of the Time Out Critics' Choice Festival at the BAC in London, was nominated for Best Show For Children And Young People at the TMA awards and also for a Race in the Media Award as a result of its broadcast on the World Service in June 2002. In 2002, UK Arts International produced the play and toured it nationally with a new cast: Jenny Platt as Margate Hannah and Erin Brodie as Kosovan Hanna. In 2003 and 2004, UK Arts International sent the play on two further extensive national tours with Louise Fitzgerald as Margate Hannah and Beth Cooper as Kosovan Hanna. The British Council also toured the play three times to the Far East. *Hannah and Hanna* has been translated and performed in Hebrew, Swedish and French (published in Editions La Fontaine, Lille, November 2004), and was staged in Holland and Portugal in 2006. It will be performed in Germany in 2007/8.

Act One

*The floor of the stage is painted to represent the wooden planking of a seaside pier. Upstage is a picture signifying Margate, displayed in such a way that other pictures can be easily substituted for it as the play proceeds. Below the picture is a narrow ledge at sitting height. There are two wooden boxes on stage, each about the size of an average suitcase; when the play begins these are side by side upstage, forming a platform. An operational karaoke machine with the name 'Hannah' on it in large capitals stands on the platform. To either side of the stage are two screens, behind which are the props that **HANNAH** and **HANNA** bring on to the stage, each of them having their own nominated screen and not using the other. Across the front of the stage (and up the sides if a thrust stage is being used) are pier railings; two identical baseball caps hang on these.*

SCENE 1

Margate. Summer 1999.

*The lights come up. **HANNAH** and **HANNA** enter from opposite sides of the stage. **HANNAH** is English, brassily made up, with her hair up; **HANNA**, Kosovan, is plainly dressed and wears no make-up. Each has photographs that they show the audience in turn during the following.*

HANNAH   That's Margate from my window.

HANNA   That's Pristina, from the window of my old house.
Pristina is the capital city of Kosovo.

HANNAH   That's me on the beach.
You can't see me because it's packed.

HANNA   That's me in a truck on its way from Kosovo to Dover.
You can't see me because I am hiding in the truck.

HANNAH   That's the block of flats I live in with my nan.

HANNA   That's the window of the room which I share with my mother and my brother in the Hotel Bellevue in Margate.

HANNAH   That's my brother Joe.

He's twenty-two and already a policeman.
Ugly, ain't he?

HANNA   This is my mother.
She sits all day looking at the sea from our window.

HANNAH   And that's my bloke; everyone calls him Bullfrog –
Well, Bull to his face.

HANNA   And this is my brother Albin.
He walks around all day with the other young Kosovan guys.
They have nothing to do.
Handsome, isn't he?

HANNAH   My name is Hannah.
I'm sixteen.
I've lived in Margate all my life.
Margate – what a town!
I hate it!

HANNA   My name is Hanna.
I'm sixteen.
I've lived in Margate for three days.
Margate what a town!
I love it!

HANNAH   Summer in Margate.
July was crap.
August is scorching hot.

HANNA   This is my new home.
I fear nothing.

HANNAH   The beaches are full of bodies.
So are the hotels, four or five to a room.

HANNA   Only thing I fear is leaving Margate.
Going home.

HANNAH   But it's not like the old days.
The people on the beaches ain't the same as the people in
the hotels.

HANNA   Three months of hiding in the mountains.
Three days in a lorry to England.
It is so nice to sleep in a bed.

HANNAH   Bullfrog says 'It's a bloody invasion,

Kosovo arrived here in the night!'
That pretty much sums up the feeling locally.

HANNA   My family lost everything.
Except our freedom.
When we arrived in Dover I kissed the ground.
Free.
At last.

*HANNAH sets up the karaoke machine during the
following.*

*HANNA moves away – either staying on stage or moving
down into the audience.*

HANNAH   Picture this:
I'm down on the seafront
With Bull and all his mates,
Doing what I do best
On a hot summer night.

SCENE 2

The seafront by night.

*With some ad-lib patter HANNAH introduces 'I Should Be So Lucky'
by Kylie Minogue. She switches on the machine and sings the song
to a backing tape. All the style and gesture is precisely reproduced.
HANNAH ad-libs so the audience sees she is performing for an
onstage 'audience' with whom she interacts either to insult (in
reaction to their taunts) or flirt or show off.*

*HANNA moves towards HANNAH, watching her performance.
HANNAH spots HANNA and continues to sing. Then she stops
singing, with the tape still playing and herself still moving to the
music*

HANNAH   Are you another one of them?

HANNA is blank.

Thought you **were somehow, so**mething in the air… (*She
sniffs.*)
What can it be?
It's a sort of foreign smell – maybe it ain't you.
It must be the scum that comes in with the tide at night.

She sings again, then breaks off.

You still standing there?
Where you from then?
Outer Mongolia?

HANNA *is blank.*

Timbukbloodytoo?

HANNA *is blank.*

(*Switching off the tape.*) Don't tell me. I spy with my little eye
    someone beginning with 'K'.

HANNAH *reacts as if she has got a laugh from the 'audience'
for this.* **HANNA** *is still blank.*

K-K-K-Kosovo…?

HANNA *looks down as if ashamed.*

Haven't you got a tongue in your head?

HANNAH *takes in her friends laughing at* **HANNA**. **HANNA**
is silent.

Well, come on then Kosovan Spice, say something or
    die…

HANNA *is silent.* **HANNAH** *walks over to her and puts the
microphone to* **HANNA**'s *mouth.*

Okay, what's your name?

HANNA   My name is Hanna.

HANNAH   (*To Bull and her mates and the audience.*) That ain't her real
                name.
                They're all bloody liars.
                Don't you know that much?
                Yeah, it's so funny…
                Oh, you can all sod off.

HANNAH *goes behind her screen with a clatter, taking her
karaoke machine with her and leaving her friends behind.*

HANNA   My real name is Xhevahinja ('*Jerve-a-heera'.*)
                But no one can pronounce it here.
                My middle name is Hanna,
                So here in Margate my mother named me again.

Hanna – because of all our sorrow,
And because it would help me to make friends in England.
I didn't mean to take her name.

SCENE 3

The lights change to a different outdoor setting.

HANNAH *comes out from behind her screen.*

HANNAH   Cliftonville is a mile up from Margate.
It's all posh hotels and lawns
Looking over the sea.
There's a bowling green there
Where Bull and I always go
When it's hot and it's dark.
But I just wasn't in the mood…
I was bloody furious, wouldn't you be?
It's my name and I ain't sharing it with an asylum seeker!
Suddenly Bull's off on one –

(*As Bull.*) Bloody Kosovans.
Come over to Dover.
Nick yer house, your car, your girlfriend,
Load their trolleys up for nothing
And get a hundred pound a week –
For what? To have a lovely seaside holiday for a year!
We should be so lucky.
That Kosovitch!
I'd tell her straight –
Go back home –
'N' give her a slap next time.

(*As **HANNAH**.*) That's my boy!
I'm the only Hannah round here aren't I?

She reacts as if Bull is walking towards her.

Come here, Bull. Where would I be without you?

HANNAH *returns behind her screen.*

HANNA   I go home and I am upset because the English don't like me.
Mother is crying in our room.
The sun is shining and she's crying.

My brother won't stay in our room.
He does not like her crying.
He goes out on the street all the day.
He walks in a gang to be safe.
Kosovan gang – English gang – very bad.
I don't like this English girl
But I like how she sings.

Pause.

I sing too.
I know all the songs as well as her.
Everyone in Pristina knows English music.
I like Britney Spears, All Saints, Westlife, Celine Dion, Steps.

HANNA sings 'Tragedy' by Steps for a full minute, voice and gesture perfect, with no accompaniment.

Some people here are stupid.
They don't like us here but they don't know us;
But Joe the policeman who protects our hotel,
He is smiling and makes jokes.
He makes us feel safe.
I am going to make the shopping
In Aldi's.

HANNA goes behind her screen.

HANNAH comes out from behind her screen wearing an Aldi's overall. She sets up the counter at Aldi's supermarket by moving the two boxes and turning them onto their ends. She stands behind the counter; till operations etc are mimed.

The lights change to an indoor setting.

HANNAH   Aldi's: it's where I work on Saturday and Thursday nights.
Everyone goes there.
It's the cheapest shop in Margate.
Last Thursday, I'm standing here behind the counter,
There's a massive queue
It's one of our busiest nights.

HANNA comes out from behind her screen wearing a cheap anorak and carrying a supermarket basket and shopping voucher. She stands as if queuing.

And guess who is holding everyone up?
(*To **HANNA**.*) Got an Aldi's card?

HANNA   No.

HANNAH   Cashback?

HANNA   No. (*She holds out the voucher.*)

HANNAH   (*Peering at **HANNA**'s basket.*) You can only spend ten pounds
with one of these you know.
You can't buy the whole shop.

HANNA   I have vouchers for myself, my brother and my mother.
That's thirty pounds.

HANNAH   Your mother and brother here are they?

HANNA   No, they are at home.

HANNAH   Where's that, then?

HANNA   Here, in Margate. I live here, you know.

HANNAH   I thought your home was in Kosovo.
Margate's my home, not yours.
You people just don't seem to realise that,
However many times you're told it,
Do you?

HANNA   I came here to buy food, not listen again to you.
Please stop your talking.

HANNAH   One voucher buys ten pounds of shopping,
No change.
One person one voucher per week.
You'll have to put it back
Or bring the rest of the family in.
Call them on your mobile.

HANNA   I have not got a mobile.

HANNAH   You've all got mobiles.

HANNA   I have no phone, I have no pounds.
I take the bread, the butter, the jam, the apples, the oranges,
the coffee, the sugar, the oil, the ham, the shampoo – seven
pounds and five p; the banana, the washing powder, the
aspirin, the Coke – nine pounds and fifty-seven p.

HANNAH No change.

HANNA The baked beans.

HANNAH Nine pounds and eighty p,
Get some matches and start a fire.

HANNA You have the money,
Why don't you set fire to yourself?

HANNAH and *HANNA* *walk downstage and face the audience.*

She has no right to talk to me like that.

HANNAH You'd think she owned the bloody place the way she carries on.

HANNA A lady in the queue said at least I stood up for myself.

HANNAH Next time I won't give her the chance.

They exit.

SCENE 4

The seafront by night.

HANNAH *comes on with her karaoke machine and sets it up. She then repeats exactly the ad-lib patter she used to introduce the Kylie Minogue song in Scene 2 and sings 'Baby One More Time' by Britney Spears with the karaoke machine to the same crowd that she did Kylie for.*

HANNA *comes out from behind her screen and joins in, singing along really well and successfully for a sustained period until* *HANNAH* *can stand it no longer and stops singing. The karaoke machine continues playing.*

HANNAH Shut up! I don't want to sing with you, talk to you
Or live in the same bloody town as you!
I don't want to breathe the same air as you people
So go away and stop stalking me round,
You freaky foreign person.
I don't want to see you again –
Alright?

HANNA *stares at* *HANNAH.*

Don't stand there pretending you're a human.
You're Kosovan, that's a foreign word, means scum.

HANNA turns and very slowly returns behind the screen.

(*Turning to her audience.*) Well, what are you all staring at?
No surrender.
Like you said, eh, Bull?

*HANNAH sits down and stares, then goes behind her screen
with the karaoke machine.*

*HANNAH comes out from behind her screen, running her
fingers slowly along the railings.*

*HANNAH brings out a chair and places it on stage during
the following, returning behind her screen.*

HANNA   I am in England and I'm crying.
I tell my mother what happened;
She holds me in her arms
And then she makes me sit down and she talks to me.
She sits upright in her chair, like this.

*In the course of the following she 'becomes' her mother
and sits in the chair.*

It's very hot so she's fanning herself.
The manager still hasn't fixed the window.
She talks to me a bit like a doctor talking to a patient.

The lights change to a different indoor setting

That's what she is in Pristina, a doctor.
This is what she says to me, in our language – in Albanian.
(*As her mother.*) As you know, your father loved the English
  language,
But most of all he loved the English people.
English was his life and his work;
He taught the language very well
And after the Serbs sacked him
He had only one student left –
You, his darling girl.
But there is one thing you must not forget:
Your father could talk all day about England –
Westminster, Brighton Pier, FA Cup, Tony Blair –

But he never came to England.
He never left Kosovo!
Unlike you, he never saw the sea,
Only mountains.
You know what I'm saying, don't you?
Kosovo was invaded and crushed for ten years.
He would say 'The *English* would never let this happen to
   England !'
Your father imagined the English to be so good,
So honourable, so courageous, so decent.
Well, of course
There never was a people like that anywhere…
I don't like the English who call us names
And if your father was alive and in Margate,
Neither would he.

(*As herself.*) It's no use listening to my mother.
She thinks in Kosovan.
What am I supposed to do?
Stay in all day?

*HANNA goes behind her screen, taking the chair. During the
following, she returns with a different chair for HANNAH's
nan, then goes behind her screen again.*

*HANNAH comes out with a laundry bag, a pile of library
books and a newspaper.*

The lights change to a different indoor setting.

HANNAH   I go home.
I'm churned up.
Just who does she think she is?
I've never been as hard as that before on anyone…
I had this sickly feeling in my gut…

She acts out the following.

I stop on the way at the library and get Nan's books.
Nan's who I live with because me mum ain't around.
I pick up the washing from the launderette.
Almost forget her paper.
Climb eleven floors with the washing and the books,
'Cause the lift still ain't fixed.

(*As herself, to Nan.*) Hallo, Nan.

(*Imagining Nan's reply.*) Course it's me who else is it gonna
    be?

(*As herself, to the audience.*) Nan's sitting in the corner of
    the room.
Curtains drawn as usual.
The room smells of – I dunno –
But it smells.
I give her her paper.

(*To Nan.*) Nan, you've got to start going out again;
It's beautiful outside.
You look like a ghost.

(*To the audience.*) Tell you the truth
I can't stand being in the place with her.
But Joe's busy and if I don't do the necessaries
She'd fade away in her chair.
All you'd see is the *Margate Gazette*.
Muggers, drivers, robbers, pram-pushers 'n' dog-walkers
She's afraid of them all.

(*As Nan.*) Hannah!
They've put my letter in the paper.
The one about the pensioners.
The *Margate Gazette* is a good paper, you know.
They've put my letter near the top
By a picture of the Home Secretary.
'Is he listening to Margate?' it says.

(*As herself, to Nan.*) Yeah, lovely, Nan.
But don't you think it's more important that you go out?

(*To the audience.*) She's about to lecture me about why she
    lives indoors all the time
But instead my brother Joe makes a visit
Looking very smart in his uniform.
As usual, he says:

(*As Joe.*) Don't go up to Cliftonville tonight, Hannah, I'm
    telling you.
There'll be trouble and I don't want you involved –
Right?

(*As herself.*) Right you are, Joe, never trust me, do you?

She moves Nan's chair to one side.

(*To the audience.*) Course I'll be there.

Fatboy Slim's 'Right Here Right Now' plays under the following.

It's Saturday night.
Keep me head low from Joe –
He can smell smoke on me breath at fifty paces.
In this town trouble's a magnet.
What else is there to look for in Margate?
It's a year-round rumble for having to live in the place –
And now we can hit Kosovans
'Stead of each other.
I wanna go there.
So I'll end up there,
Joe or no Joe –
Magnetic, see?

The volume of the music rises.

HANNA *comes on; she and* **HANNAH** *perform a choreo-graphed dance sequence representing a street fight. The music ends.*

SCENE 5

The lights change to an outdoor setting.

HANNA   Saturday night in Cliftonville.

HANNAH   Same street.

HANNA   Same wall.

HANNAH   Same aggro bubbling under.
Bull's there. Finished work at six,
Had four pints by eight.
It's a hot night;
He's in shorts, shades,
And a shirt with 'Kosoville' on it in letters of dripping blood.

HANNA   Albin and his friends are bored of being told to go home.
They decide to walk across the road,
Play a football game.

HANNAH   Nine-a-side,
                  Shirts for goal posts;
                  Stripped to the waist 'n' off they go.
                  Kosovan asylum seeker team A versus Kosovan asylum
                        seeker team B.

  HANNA   The Kosovans play football very good.
                  All the girls see that, so the boys do too, I know.

HANNAH   Nothing happens, we're quite happy to watch the game.
                  Then whose idea is it to nick the bloody ball?

  HANNA   Her stupid ugly boyfriend runs on to the grass,
                  Puts the ball under his arm and runs towards the cliff.

HANNAH   Off goes Bull followed by eighteen Kosovan lads,
                  Each one bare-chested and with a knife in his pocket,
                  Screaming blue murder, in Albanian,
                  Chased by another thirty Margate kids;
                  Then two coppers, screaming into the radiophones for help...

  HANNA   Ugly boy reaches the clifftop,
                  Kicks the ball up into the air,
                  Down into the sea below.

HANNAH   Hang on, the ball goes up into the air
                  But not down into the sea.
                  It hovers,
                  Seems to stop and have a think,
                  Changes its mind
                  And falls onto the tarmac into the middle of fifty panting
                        youths.

  HANNA   Albin jumps up and catches it
                  And off he goes running like the wind,
                  Back over the grass,
                  Across the road
                  Down Ethelred Crescent –
                  Fifty of us chasing the ball in Albin's hands –
                  Why?
                  I don't *know* why
                  But I can't stop running...

HANNAH   Bull's running across the tops of cars –
                  His favourite trick.

The dog-walkers and pram-pushers dive for cover
And a lady with a stick goes flying across the pavement.
Someone screams and there's a crash of glass.
On we go,
Into the road;
Cars screech out the way.

HANNA & HANNAH CRASH!

HANNA The car hits the lamp-post and stops,
The post like this.
I don't stop,
I don't care, I just run and run,
Faster now,
Down the hill;
There's more than fifty of us now.

HANNAH A bus swerves;
It nearly, oh-so-nearly, goes flat upon its side.
You should have heard the screams inside.
Loud enough to wake the dead of Margate.

HANNA We turn a corner and I see the beach, the bay, the lights.
Many, many people too.
For one second I see Albin
Still in front, his face a knife;
Then on he goes, he's gone.

HANNAH I turn round for a second,
Look behind;
In the dying light I see 'bout eighty of 'em
And I'm telling you
For one second I thought:
'If the Kosovans need Margate,
Then Margate needs the Kosovans!
When last did we have such a time as *this*?'

HANNA Faster and faster
Down the hill to the beach. I can't stop running.
My legs are moving faster;
I can't stop my legs.
On to the sand.

HANNAH We hit the beach.
The Kosovan with the ball stops.

HANNA Albin kicks it in the air.

HANNAH It lands in the sea and bobs about on the tide.

HANNA The stupidest fight you've ever seen begins.

HANNA & HANNAH All in slow motion.

HANNAH The breath has gone from everybody
The sand soaks up the action.

They flop.

HANNA (*Her hands on her knees, breathing heavily; alert.*)
Ugly boy is moving through the gasping bodies.
He's moving towards Albin.
Albin doesn't see him.

HANNAH I look up to see Bull land a heavy punch
To the head of the Kosovan who carried the ball.

HANNAH He drops like a stone.
Everyone around Bull's cheering.
Bull's goin' mad.

HANNA He's kicking Albin in the head.
Albin!

HANNAH Bull! What d'ya think you're doing!

HANNA (*Screaming.*) Albin!

HANNAH (*Screaming.*) Bull!

They both run towards Bull and mime attempting to pull him off Albin.

HANNA & HANNAH Get off get off get off.

HANNAH turns and reacts as if seeing her brother.

HANNA 'sees' the policeman who visited her hotel.

HANNA Look, it's the policeman from our hotel…
Look! Look!

HANNAH Joe! Joe! Pull him off before he kills him!

They mime pulling Bull off Albin, their actions stylized and identical.

Joe had him in an arm-lock and out of view in seconds flat. I
saw him and a woman copper take him off.

HANNA   Albin was still bleeding from his nose and head. (*She turns to address **HANNAH**.*) Please… Hannah…

                     ***HANNAH** turns reluctantly to **HANNA**.*

                     Please help me lift him up.
                     I have to take him home.

HANNAH   You'll never get him back up to Cliftonville.
                     We've just run a mile and a half downhill.
                     Just wait for an ambulance.

HANNA   If they think he's making all this trouble
                     They put him in prison till he goes back to Kosovo.
                     Please please help.
                     It's your boyfriend who beat him.

HANNAH   (*To the audience.*) There was fighting all around us and screaming.
                     Her brother started groaning.
                     I said

                     (*To **HANNA**.*) Okay. My flat's crap but it's near the beach.
                     Come with me.

HANNA   I will. Thank you Hannah.

HANNAH   (*To the audience.*) Sometimes you just have to grit your teeth, don't you?

SCENE 6

Groove Armada's 'By the River' plays.

The lights change to a different outdoor setting.

***HANNA** takes a bandanna from her pocket and ties it round her head to become Albin. **HANNAH** carries **HANNA**/Albin around the stage and onto one of the boxes (representing the tower block). **HANNAH** mimes pressing the bell of the intercom.*

HANNAH   (*To Nan, into the intercom.*) Hi, Nan, it's me.
                     No, I've got my key.
                     I'm just bringing two visitors up, okay?
                     No, you don't know them.
                     One of them's hurt, okay?
                     Is the lift…?

Good!
(*To the audience.*) We put him in the lift; I was shaking.

*The lights change to an indoor setting. **HANNAH** and **HANNA**
step down from the box. Nan's chair is moved centre.*

We get to my door.
Nan's standing there.
She screams her head off.
I ain't ever heard her scream before.
Goes to her room
And slams the door.

The music ends.

HANNA   (*To the audience.*) We made Albin comfortable.
Then we saw each other. We were both covered in blood.
(*To **HANNAH**.*) Keep him awake.
I won't be long.

HANNAH   (*To **HANNA**.*) Where are you going?

HANNA   To get my mother. She knows what to do.

HANNAH   You can't leave me here…

***HANNA** goes behind her screen.*

(*To the audience.*) The front door slams.
She's gone.
Nan's door opens.
Her head peeps round.

(*As Nan.*) Have they gone?

(*As herself.*) – she says.
Out she comes,
Slap into Albin
Bleeding over her favourite chair.
I almost died.
She didn't move or say nothing.
Then,

(*As Nan.*) We better clean the poor sod up, hadn't we?
His mother can't see him like this.

(*As herself.*) And she takes over, fussing over Albin – he was
   Albin now –

Like he was her own.
She dabbed and wiped.
Albin groaned in pain.
Then the buzzer went.

HANNA comes out as her mother, no longer wearing the bandanna and carrying a handbag.

HANNA (*To the audience.*) My mother walks in.

HANNAH She's not what I expected;
No headscarf, no anorak.
She smells of nice perfume.
She's quite a lady.
She checks over Albin very professional
Then gives him a *big* cuddle.
She smiles at Nan, who almost curtsies;
Then Hanna's mother tries to thank my nan.

HANNA (*As her mother, to Nan.*) You – very – good – English
– dame.

HANNAH Before
Nan thought Kosovans were all a bunch of hooligans.

(*As Nan, to Mother.*) Your English ain't up to much is it, love?

(*To the audience.*) She's very impressed.
Offers her a cup of tea.

HANNA (*As her mother.*) Thank you, madam.

HANNAH Then Joe turns up and is about to start on me.
Nan cuts in, quite posh.
'Don't start now, Joe,
We've got some visitors from abroad.'

HANNA (*To the audience.*) We see the figure of a policeman at the
door.
The asylum seekers turn to stone.
We feel guilty.
It's automatic.
So crazy.
Hanna's grandmother introduces him as Joe, her grandson.
It's him.
The policeman from our hotel.

The policeman on the beach.
The angel policeman.
Albin nods to him, very polite.
Mother shakes his hand.
I stand staring like I do.

HANNAH   I'm getting this sickly feeling in my gut again.
I feel dizzy.

HANNA   I'm glad to be here.
Everyone safe.
Albin is on his feet.
Mother smiling.
And I've found Hannah.
Without even looking for her.
She's standing by the doorway now –
I can't see her face…

HANNAH   I watch them sitting, three Kosovans,
An angry pensioner and a policeman…
Why can't I let go and enjoy the party too?

HANNA   I translate for Albin and for my mother.
Her name is Flora which makes them laugh
Because in England it means margarine.
Hannah's grandmother asked us if we will come back next
     Friday
And of course my mother says we will.
This is the first time my mother has left the hotel
Since we arrived.
The first time she has used
The English that she knows.
Albin doesn't speak
But I know he understands.
He is quiet with the policeman.
It was Albin who had the ball.
After some time we say goodbye and thank you.
Many times.
Hannah comes out of the shadow.

(*To* **HANNAH**.) Do you mind if I come and see you again?

HANNAH   Yeah,
We'll do a song or something in my room, okay?

HANNA   Thank you, Hannah.

HANNAH   (*To the audience.*) Go on, hate me, I do.
          I just wanted to do something,
          Something nice like everyone else seemed to be doing.
          And it made my stomach feel better,
          So it was the right thing
          For me to do
          At the time.
          Right?

          'Torn' by Natalie Imbruglia plays over the theatre speakers.
          HANNAH *and* ***HANNA*** *sing to the CD. This is a turning point*
          for them; they take some time to thaw out, and though the
          singing is good it takes until the end of the song for the girls
          to be at ease with each other.

HANNA   What do you want to be when you grow up?

HANNAH   I wanna be rich.
          What do you want to be?

HANNA   I want to be a pharmacist.

          The music fades.

HANNAH   (*To the audience.*) All this leaves out Bullfrog.
          I couldn't tell him about Hanna and me.
          He'd turn into a one-man mental institution.
          I liked him.
          Till that night on the beach
          When he tasted blood.
          Once Hanna walked past me and Bull on the front
          And I had to do it.
          I had to pretend I was the same as I was before.

          (*Shouting directly at* ***HANNA***.) Kosovo. Scum. Go home.

          HANNAH *and* ***HANNA*** *both turn to face the audience.*

          I'm so sorry.
          I had to do that.
          I'm so sorry, Hanna.

HANNA   It's okay. In my country it happens all the time.

          HANNAH *and* ***HANNA*** *move to opposite sides of the stage*

HANNAH   Things have changed.
         Me and Hanna are like Nan now.

HANNA   Like Nan *was*.

HANNAH   Oh yeah.
         She goes out now.
         All by herself.

HANNA   My mum and Albin and Joe all meet for tea on Fridays.

HANNAH   My nan's started the Kosovan branch of the Women's
           Institute…
         If Bull finds out
         I'll be the one needing asylum.

HANNA   (*Of HANNAH.*) She worries too much.
         I love being in her flat.
         Eleven floors up looking over the sea.
         We are singing every day.
         No one can see us.
         No one can hear us.

         *HANNAH and HANNA change their positions to indicate a
         passage of time.*

HANNAH   It was getting boring, staying in.
         So we went out,
         Sang on the front.
         Bull was there.
         But I weren't bothered.
         We just sung
         Our favourite song.

         *HANNAH urges the anxious HANNA onto the box platform.
         They sing and dance a perfected, unaccompanied version of
         'Perfect' by Fairground Attraction. This is a real performance
         piece the girls have worked on for weeks.*

         *HANNAH and HANNA become Bull, taking the caps from
         the railing, putting them on and speaking in unison to the
         audience.*

HANNAH & HANNA (*As Bull.*) Gotcha!
         Asylum lover.
         Kosovo lesbo.

Margate bloody traitor.
English scum.
You come out on the front again,
You're dead.
Hear that,
You're dead.
Hannah,
Bloody Hannah:
Dead,
Right?
Dead.

HANNAH and HANNA exit separately.

Act Two

SCENE 1

The Margate picture upstage has been replaced by one depicting a grey sea with seagulls. The railings and the chairs have been removed. The boxes are on their sides with a gap between them; the props for Act Two are brought from the boxes rather than from behind the screens.

*When Act Two begins, **HANNAH** – now in drab clothes, with no make-up and her hair down – and **HANNA** are on stage in darkness. The lights come up on them.*

HANNAH (*To the audience.*) One night, just before Christmas,
Bull and his mates – his 'bully-boys' as he likes to call 'em –
They ambushed us as we came out the main door of the
flats.
It was me they wanted to hurt, not Hanna.

*A piano version of 'Good King Wenceslas' plays. In a choreographed sequence, **HANNAH** is spat at, kicked and trodden on by **HANNA** as Bull. The music ends.*

During the following scene, each keeps to her side of the stage as they are in separate rooms.

HANNA (*As herself, to the audience.*) I sit in the library because it is
warm and I read English books.
We don't meet anymore, not even in secret.
Hannah is hurt.
She is afraid of Bull now.
I know very well how she is feeling
But I miss her.
I haven't seen her for days.

HANNAH I've stopped going out just for the time being.
It's pretty horrible out there anyway.
Joe keeps an eye on our door, which is nice.
When the lift broke again I asked Joe not to get it fixed.
I feel safer up here that way.
Anyway, whenever I been out lately I was getting 'English
scum, asylum-lover',

All that crap in my ears.
And it weren't just me: Joe got it too.
Once word got out about Nan's Friday tea-parties.
He had the piss taken once too often.
Joe ended up in a fight himself over it.
Nan didn't like both of us getting grief;
So she closed down the tea-parties.
Now Nan moans at *me* for never going out.
But she looks after me
Like I looked after her.
When the rain beats on the windows all through the
      afternoon
All I can see is grey shite and seagulls.

A piano version of Nina Simone's 'Little Girl Blue' plays.

I've started going through my mum's old vinyls.
It cheers me up.
Nan says my mum was a bit of a singer,
Into all kinds of music.
Folk, jazz, you name it.
I never listened to it before.
Some of the stuff in here is alright.
I learn the ones I really like,
Put them on a tape.
Nan delivers the tape – plus my letter – to Hanna,
Then Nan stops and talks to Flora for about nine hours.
Gawd knows what they got to talk about
Considering they hardly understand one another.
By the time she leaves
Hanna's already written me her letter back.

HANNA   I am learning the new songs in bed, sometimes in the dark.
The manager says there are too many heaters in the hotel;
If you turn one on, all the lights go off,
So it's cold and that's why I am in bed.

*HANNAH and HANNA collect Walkman headphones from
the boxes and put them on. They sing 'Little Girl Blue' as if
they are singing along to a tape.*

The music ends.

*HANNAH sits on her box, staring downstage as if through a
window, then takes a letter from the box and opens it. She
reads it and acts it out as HANNA recites it.*

Mother stays in all day now.
I cannot make her go out.
She cannot work here even though she is a children's doctor.
Mother and Albin get more and more sad together.
I listen to your tape and I can't hear them talking,
When the weather is very bad,
I take the Walkman to the beach.
With the rain in my face
I forget everyone and everything.
I try and see you at your window
But it's too far away.
Maybe you can see me.
When I get in from the storm outside
The room feels warmer.
Mother and Albin are sleeping.
They sleep hours every day.
Dreaming of leaving,
Dreaming of home.
Happy Millennium, Hannah.

*They sing part of Abba's 'Mamma Mia' without accom-
paniment and with headphones, each in their own world.*

*HANNAH takes a '2000' hairband out of her box, puts it
on and again stares downstage as if out of the window.
HANNA takes a party popper from her box and lets it off,
then produces and opens a letter. She reads the letter as
HANNAH recites it.*

HANNAH   Happy Millennium, Hanna!
          Bull is sending nasty stuff in the mail.
          Really evil stuff, some of it.
          I don't know what's happened to his sense of humour.
          He's obsessed.
          And since things are quieter at your hotel,
          Joe spends more time keeping an eye on my door
          Than he does on yours.
          Bull seems to think I'm the asylum seeker now

So it's me who gets the treatment
'Cause I don't hate you.
He hates me.
It's stupid and it's doing my bloody head in.
Every time I think I'll go out,
I wanna be sick
But I'll keep writing
And sending you the tapes, just for now.
Joe got into trouble for that scrap I told you about.
Nearly lost his job.
Coppers can't get into punch-ups.
It's illegal.
He's going to do something about it, he says,
But he won't say what.

(*As Joe.*) You'll see –

(*As herself.*) – he says –

(*As Joe.*) – you'll see.

(*As herself.*) The longer I stay in
The harder it is to go out…
I'll come and see you soon.
Promise.
PS: Do you like that song by the A-Teens?
I hope you like it as much as I do.

The A-Teens' 'Mamma Mia' plays at a low volume. **HANNAH**
and **HANNA** *make a series of tableaux to show the months
passing.*

HANNA & HANNAH January. February. March. April.

*The music increases in volume. They dance to 'Mamma
Mia', each still in their own separate room, with great
emotion,* **HANNA** *liberated,* **HANNAH** *raging. The music
volume drops.* **HANNAH** *opens a letter that* **HANNA** *speaks
as 'Mamma Mia' continues underneath.*

HANNA I have big news!
Joe is driving a lorry to Pristina.
He is taking medicines to hospitals
And as my mother is a doctor,
She may be allowed to go with him!
And Albin!

And *me*!
I don't want to go back to bloody Kosovo!
But nobody listens to me!

HANNAH   (*To the audience.*) Nan always said,
Joe's a good deed.
And you're a bad deed.
Bloody Joe.
(*To **HANNA**.*) Joe!

> *During the following, **HANNA** moves around the set as Joe, moving and fixing things as she speaks, getting ready for the journey.*

HANNA   (*As Joe.*) What?

HANNAH   You didn't tell me!

HANNA   (*As Joe.*) What?

HANNAH   This! (*She waves the letter.*)

HANNA   (*As Joe.*) Sorry… I had to ask them first, didn't I?

HANNAH   You can't leave me alone in Margate!

HANNA   (*As Joe.*) People miss you, you know that?

HANNAH   I don't miss them.

HANNA   (*As Joe.*) You can't lock yourself up in here for ever.
You gotta face the world again, Hannah.

> *HANNA takes a letter from her box and gives it to **HANNAH**. **HANNAH** opens it.*

HANNA   (*Reciting the letter.*) We are leaving next week.
My mother is so happy she can't stop smiling.
I want to see you to say goodbye.

HANNAH   Thing is, somehow, we're best friends.
Even though I never see Hanna
I can't face not seeing her again.

HANNA   Can we meet by the clock-tower at twelve tomorrow?

HANNAH   (*To the audience.*) I know it's stupid, but like my nan,
I've built up this fear of going out.
Of course, like her, I'll go out and I won't see what I fear;
I won't see Bull or his mates.
I'll just walk up to the clock-tower and we'll jump about

And then we'll go up to the hotel together
And I'll wave them off to Kosovo.
Sad how I feel jealous of an asylum seeker
For leaving Margate…
I used to think they were lucky to be here.

HANNAH exits.

HANNA changes the picture back to Margate and moves both boxes to one side.

The volume of the music comes up again for the finale.

HANNAH enters wearing a jacket and carrying a rucksack, looking fresh, herself again.

I go out.
It's a hot spring day like you get now –
The sea and the sun hit me like I'm in Spain
Or some other place I've never been to.
I feel fabulous
Like Hanna said she felt when she got here last summer.
Nan has put some sandwiches in a bag
Like I'm going on a picnic and made me promise
I'll be home by four.
'Don't worry,' I said, 'I'll probably be home for lunch.'
And eat them on the sofa.

(*As Nan.*) You'll eat them alone –

(*As herself.*) – she said –

(*As Nan.*) – I'm out today.

(*As herself.*) She's never in these days, my nan.
As I walk along the front I feel I'm flying.
Here I am, free again and newly born.
A second later I hear the chant I hate and fear:

HANNA & HANNAH Kosovans go home, go back home! –

HANNAH – 'cept this time it isn't just Bull,
        But what sounds like a pub full of monster blokes.
        My stomach churns with fear.
        I feel I'm being told to go back home.
        Instantly, I want to run back to the flat.
        I turn round and there they are,
        The National Front in triumph straggling along Sea Road.

They've brought kiddies too – boy Nazis and toy Nazis,
Even a little pushchair Nazi crying his eyes out,
All bellowing down the front at no one in particular,
Just a load of coppers and bored Margate people staring.
I'm standing there
Taking this in
And I hear –

HANNA & HANNAH Out, out, out!

HANNAH – chanted from behind me.
Yes, it's the other mob, the Anti-Nazi League,
Coming towards me!
They're arm in arm, all shapes and sizes,
And in the front line –
My nan!
The Kosovans have turned my family inside out!
Joe going there today in a truck,
Nan fighting the National Front.
What have I been doing all winter?
I want to help Nan or save her or something.
But when I look at her
Her head held high and her looking so proud
I want to hide away again.
I turn and run.
In panic I slip,
Arse over tit in the path of the National Front,
And I'm looking up at Bull.
Ugly bastard in a T-shirt
With a union jack turned into a bloody swastika across the
    front,
Yelling:

HANNA & HANNAH (*As Bull.*) England for the English!

HANNAH (*As herself, to the audience.*) A second later he'd see me.
This time I get in first.

She mimes kicking him in the crotch.

Crunch!
He went:

(*As Bull.*) England for the – aargh!

(As herself, to the audience.) I heard but I didn't see.
I was gone.

Alice DJ's 'Are You Better Off Alone?' plays loudly and continues quietly through the following.

HANNAH *exits.*

HANNA *takes a long-sleeved top from her box and ties it round her waist.*

HANNA *(Jumping up and down as if by a lamp-post, wanting to see and not be seen; to the audience.)* It's twelve o' clock and there is a war starting around me.
This is the place we said we'd meet.
Hannah, hurry, please, hurry Hannah.

HANNAH *enters and runs past **HANNA**.*

Hannah!

The music surges.

*The two girls dance and mime a long chase. During the chase they move the boxes to form a lorry: one box is laid on its side upstage to form the back, the other flat in front of it to form the cab; both are at an angle across the stage. **HANNAH** and **HANNA** also change the Margate picture to one showing complete blackness.*

The music finishes abruptly.

HANNAH *hides behind the upstage box. She is not seen by **HANNA**.*

SCENE 2

HANNA *(To the audience.)* I've lost her.
She's not at the hotel.
She's not by the lorry.
Joe is shouting at me that we're leaving now.
Mother and Albin are waving at me.
The National Front are coming up the hill.
I don't want to leave.
I don't want to leave.

The lighting changes; the front and the back portions of the lorry are illuminated, with darkness between them.

HANNA *sits down in the front of the lorry. The lorry departs*
with both girls aboard.

We've left.
We're going down the hill
In a lorry with 'Kosovo Aid' written along its side.
Spit hits the window by my head.
I look at the beach and sea for a last second.
I'm looking everywhere for Hannah.
We drive past the back of the sign that says
'Welcome to Margate'.
She's gone.
I can't see her.
I've lost her.
Where was she running?
Why was she running from me?

HANNAH   (*Emerging from behind the box; to the audience.*)
I can't see a thing in here.
It's totally black.
I want to scream my bloody head off,
But then I'd give myself away.
No one's going to find me here.
No one.

HANNA   Dover.
I remember Dover.
Three days and three nights in a lorry to get here.
We were hidden in the back all that time.
There were twelve of us and a baby.
The mother had put her hand over his mouth
Every time we stopped.
There was a hole in the top for light
A hole in the floor for toilet.
We paid three thousand pounds to come to Dover;
Everything that my father had left to us.
When the door opened on the third night
We put up our hands.
We thought we would be shot.
The man said, 'Get out now', and we did;
Then he drove away.
I did not know what country we were standing in
Till I saw the sign for Dover.

HANNAH   I've been sleeping for hours.
I don't know what time it is.
I finished the sandwiches a long time ago.
I've kept the chocolate for emergency.
But I'm starving.
There's a plastic bin to pee in,
But no lid.
Nan will be home now.
She'll think I'm a dirty stop-out.

HANNA   Calais, Dunkirk, Zeebrugge, Ghent,
Brussels, Aachen, Cologne, Frankfurt.
Albin is driving now.
Mother wants me to sing but I can't.
I left my voice in Margate.
Everything I want to forget
I remember like yesterday.
Nuremberg, Passau, Graz, Leibnitz…

HANNAH sings a verse of Bob Dylan's 'Shelter from the Storm', unaccompanied.

HANNAH   (*Speaking.*) Chocolate's gone. I'm so hungry
So hungry.
So hungry.

HANNA sings the next verse.

HANNA   (*Speaking.*) Joe says, 'My mother used to sing that! How do you know it?'
I say:
When Hannah was alone in the flat
She learnt many old songs.
Your Nan brought them to me on cassettes.
While Nan listened to Mother talking,
I learnt them.
If Hannah was here
We could sing a whole concert.
Mother says:

(*As her mother.*) Your Nan helped me very much, Joe.
She made me talk of everything until I stopped crying.
That's why we're going home now.

(*As herself, to the audience.*) Joe and Mother tell me to sing
more.
I want to sleep.
I want to go backwards.
I want to wake up again in Dover.

*They sing another verse and chorus of 'Shelter from the
Storm'.*

HANNAH   I'm turning into a cockroach in here,
A blind, dirty thing that lives in the dark.
I'm not coming out.
I'm not coming out.
They can lock me up or beat me up
But I'm going all the way.

HANNA   We stop, we start again, on and on and on.
We are always crossing borders.
I go to sleep in Hungary, wake in Romania…
The lorry is moving but I am not moving.
I am sleeping in the Hotel Bellevue,
Dreaming we are driving,
Driving…dreaming…

(*As her mother*) Wake up, Hanna, wake up!

(*As herself.*) My mother is shaking me.

*HANNA wakes up, doesn't know what's happening, where
she is.*

(*As her mother.*) Look! Kosovo!

(*As herself.*) I've been stuck so long in my seat
I don't know that we are moving.
I open the door to step out of the lorry.
My mother grabs on to my coat.
I am falling out of my coat.
Joe is shouting and stopping the lorry.
I fall out of my coat into the road.
I don't want to be in Kosovo.
Let me out, let me out, let me out!

She falls to her knees, crying and sobbing.

HANNAH   I was thrown out of my corner into the darkness.
The toilet bucket spilt over.

I was wet through.
I can't stand it anymore.
Let me out, let me out, let me out!

She falls to her knees.

HANNAH & HANNA Let me out, let me out!

HANNAH The big doors open and there's Joe.

(*As Joe.*) Hannah! What the fuck are you doing here?

(*As herself.*) Oh Joe, I'm seeking asylum from Margate.

HANNAH & HANNA And there was Hanna(h).

A lyrical Kosovan folk melody plays, very loud.

HANNAH and HANNA go mental and jump around the stage together in delight, shouting out each other's name.

The music decreases in volume. The girls eventually fall silent and embrace.

HANNAH We washed in a river.
I stuffed my face with food.
Hanna lent me a clean top.

HANNA gives HANNAH the top from around her waist. HANNAH puts it on.

HANNA I was ready to jump,
But Hannah is here.
I am in Kosovo,
But Hannah is here.
I cannot believe it.
I cannot believe it.

HANNAH and HANNA change the upstage picture to one of the Kosovan landscape, then sit on the downstage box and fall asleep.

The Kosovan music continues to play. They wake.

SCENE 3

The lights change to a general state over the whole stage. HANNAH and HANNA stand centre stage, HANNA behind HANNAH.

The music fades.

HANNAH   We woke up.
      I think we woke up anyway.
      Everything seemed slower and brighter.
      I don't remember how we were standing
      By the side of the road
      And no longer in the lorry…
      That's where we were.
      It was getting dark.
      Hanna and me were staring at a coach.

HANNA   That's the coach.

HANNAH   A dead coach, you could say.
      It was all brown and black;
      Brown with rust and black from fire,
      Parked by itself on this empty road.
      Mountains all around.
      All of a sudden,
      Albin goes totally mental.
      He runs at the coach,
      Pounding the side of it with his feet and his fists,
      Bellowing and howling,
      And smashing up what's already smashed.

HANNA   We left for Macedonia in that coach;
      It was our escape from Kosovo,
      The beginning of our journey to Margate.
      We were stopped by the Serbs.
      They were selecting young people;
      Albin and I were both chosen.
      My mother was still in that coach.
      They would not let her off.
      The men were taken off first.
      The women were taken to a garage
      Twenty minutes down the road,
      A big empty building.
      The soldiers all had knives and guns;
      All were wearing masks.
      My clothes were torn off me.

      She stops.

      At some point the screaming around me stopped;
      I think the soldiers got some sort of order.

I do not know why they set us free.
We were taken out of the garage, back to the roadside.
We smelt the coach burning before we saw it.
We met up again with the men.
Albin was there and though he was beaten
He was standing.
He was alive.
I was ashamed for him to see me like this,
But he saw I was alive too.
Not all of the men were there.
The coach was still in flames.
The Serbs made us walk to Macedonia.
I did not know if my mother was dead in the coach.
When I got to the camp in Macedonia I was very bad.
My mother was waiting for us.
She was alive.
She looked after us.
She helped me not to be ashamed.
I cried for weeks and my mother said:
'Don't stop, cry more.'
And hugged me.
When Albin told me about a lorry going to England
He said it was the first time that I smiled again.
We could go to England.
Sorry to make you sad.

HANNAH says nothing.

Say something.

HANNAH says nothing.

Haven't you got a tongue in your head?

HANNAH   I'd want to kill the people who did that to me.

HANNA   That's what Albin wants to do.
That's why he's come back.
But I do not want that.

HANNAH   I feel useless.

HANNA   You're not.
You're here.

HANNAH   I called you scum.

HANNA   I fought back.

HANNAH   I feel sick.
I wish I was in Margate.

HANNA   So do I.
So much.

HANNAH   Come back.
I'm not frightened anymore
And neither should you be.
They can call us what names they bloody like.
Right?

HANNA   Right…

HANNAH   I know,
We'll sing.
Sing together.
Become a group.
Get on *Top of the Pops* or something – right?

HANNA   Right. I can't come.

HANNAH   Nan'll put you up.

HANNAH turns and faces HANNA.

HANNA   I'm not allowed back.

HANNAH   Sez who?

HANNA   Once you leave you can't go back. Only if I've got lots of money.
Or if I marry an English guy…

HANNAH   Marry Joe…

They laugh.

Look.
If you can't come to Margate,
I'll stay here with you for a while.
Nan can manage by herself for a bit.
Wha'd'ya say?

HANNA   Did you bring your passport?

HANNAH   Passport?
No.

I ain't got one.
I ain't never been abroad before.

HANNA drops her head.

I'm sorry about what you told me.
I'm sorry it happened to you.
I'm sorry.

HANNA   Why haven't you got a passport?
Then you could stay for a bit.
I wish I had a British passport.
I could live in Margate.
I wouldn't have to be here in Kosovo
And live with people who want to kill each other.
You don't see Margate like me.
It's a beautiful town.
One day other people will go there
And they will see it too.
(*Pointing.*) Look,
Mother and Albin are waiting for me.
Joe is waiting for you.
He still has to deliver the medicines before he takes you
    home.
Just a mile up that little road is where we sleep tonight
Before we go to Pristina;
From here we walk.

HANNAH turns and faces HANNA.

HANNAH   Is this it?

HANNA   Yes.
This is it.

*HANNAH and HANNA sing 'Torn' unaccompanied. They have
a new sound, more experimental, not gloomy, a mixture of
pop and folk.*

HANNAH and HANNA exit separately.

Blackout.

CLUB ASYLUM

for Andy Howitt

Background

Asylum seekers were relatively new to Scotland at the beginning of 2002, and the manner in which they had been tenanted overnight in schemes like Sighthill was a very sore point for a lot of residents.

But the teenagers that we dealt with, from many countries, were animated by Glasgow and liked their new home. Their fear was not of staying in the city but of leaving it. Most of them were deeply impressed by the schools – fourteen year-old Somalians and Kosovans would gravely tell you how good the education was. The special units in the schools for asylum seekers were superbly run and very welcoming; in some schools, like St Roch's, they were managed by men and women who were once refugees to Glasgow themselves. The teenage asylum seekers responded with incredible energy to these new opportunities and they brought a new intellectual standard – a new level of aspiration – into Glasgow at that time. Studies have shown that young asylum seekers under this sort of pressure out-perform teenagers from indigenous families. It is searing to realise that there is no real popular appreciation of just what the young 'asylums' have achieved by the time they are suddenly removed in a dawn raid.

There is a growing awareness now – thanks to organisations like The Glasgow Campaign to Welcome Refugees and Positive Action For Housing. The most affecting story is that of the 'Glasgow Girls' and the influence that they have brought to bear on Jack McConnell. This is a singular development – it's clear that young asylum seekers and local teenagers (or 'old and new Glaswegians') are now standing up for each other. Is this happening anywhere else in Europe? So openly and effectively? It must be one of the first indications of a new and radical intelligence emerging from the big asylum intake of 2000/1.

The exchanges and poems that make up this text can be explored in any order and there is no set way that dance and text should be performed.

In our version, all of the poetic passages were spoken chorally – the 'I' was always plural.

The rousing acclaim that the show received from the press and audiences alike suggests that we found a sound and a style that worked at the time.

Those choices are history now and a group interested to perform *Club Asylum* will choose its own sounds and choreographic style.

Characters

ST MUNGO

GLASGOW BOY 1

GLASGOW BOY 2

GLASGOW BOY 3

ASYLUM SEEKER GIRL 1

ASYLUM SEEKER GIRL 2

TEACHER

FASCIST

YOUNG ASIAN GUY

MARTIAL ARTS TEACHER

DAVOUD RASAL NASERI

With doubling or dividing of parts, this physical theatre text can be performed by any number of actors. The original production was performed by three male and two female actors. This meant that each actor played both a Glaswegian and an asylum seeker.

Club Asylum was first performed at the Tron Theatre, Glasgow, on 8 February 2002 with the following company:

Umar Ahmed
Martin Docherty
Lee Hart
Jane Howie
Cathleen McCarron

Director John Retallack
Choreographer Andy Howitt
Design / Lighting Kevin McCallum

Club Asylum was made possible by the Scottish Arts Council 'Scotland Onstage' scheme, Glasgow City Council and the Diane, Princess of Wales Memorial Fund. It was a co-production between macrobert, Scotland's leading arts centre for young people, and Company of Angels, and toured throughout Scotland in Spring 2002.

Club Asylum – and *Risk* – were both initiated by Liz Moran, the director of macrobert in Stirling and herself a true pioneer in bringing new work in all art forms to young people throughout Scotland.

Club Asylum

ST MUNGO   My mother was raped at fifteen by a Welsh crazy
My grandfather was so mad at her for getting pregnant
He threw her off a cliff one hundred metres high
In a cart.
That didn't kill her.
They towed the cart with her on it out to sea
And cast her adrift for days.
That didn't drown her.
After two days floating in the sea
The tide changed
She was hurled by the waves onto a beach.
She dragged her body across the sand
Dropped down half dead by an old campfire.
Then the birth pangs began.
There in the wilderness in a storm.
Alone and fifteen
She gave birth to me.
A man found us and took us to a priest.
The priest gave shelter to my mother
And me, he lifted up in his arms,
'Dear One' he said
Or, in the language of the day,
'Mungo'
I was a spiritual person from the day I was born.
I loved the man who saved our life
I loved the place he found us.
'Dear green place' I said
Or, in the language of the day,
'Glescu'
The founder of your city was an orphan
Or, in the language of our day,
'Refugee'

_____

GLASGOW VOICES I'm thinking of leaving Sighthill
And coming back here on a coach in the middle of the night
I'll say no speak English and come with only a plastic bag
I'll take out a dirty piece of paper
With new bathroom new kitchen written on it
I'll just show it to the one in charge
Then sit in the middle of the road and cry

Pause.

In ten minutes I'll be in my asylum flat
Painted, plumbed, all new fittings and fixtures
Very nice
Quicker than waiting for the council

They walk forward.

Wish I had a new flat
Wish I had a new kitchen
Wish I had a new bathroom
Wish I got all they got
Free
Available on arrival

Welcome to your new city
Please jump to the top of the queue
You are the new Glaswegians
You are the VIPs
The new stars of the old schemes
The ones we want to be happy
Sorry about the people you've got to live with.
If we could make them disappear
We would

Did they tell us they were coming?
Did they ask us how we felt?
Before they rushed to give them their rights
Did they check on ours?
Did they do all these good deeds for asylums,
Because they love folk from Nigeria?
Do they? Do they fuck!
There's money in the asylums
And not a penny to be made out of loving us

Glasgow City has a new club
Members get the freedom of the city
A free place in every queue
Home on demand
School on demand
Doctor on demand
Food on demand
You want it now?
It's yours Mustapha.
Did you have to wait?
Sorry Fatima
Don't speak a word of English?
Not a problem Mohammed.
You've got some family want to join you?
Say no more Mr Bongo.

Welcome to Club Asylum
Just sign the form
It's open to everyone
As long as you never lived here
Strictly off limits
To Glaswegians
No, don't worry
Your welcome pack tells you all you need to know
Here are your keys
The fridge is full
Don't mind us
Enjoy your stay
Just remember
Stay invisible
And you'll be alright

**Dance of the Glaswegians
Music: 'Operation Blade' by Public Domain**

GLASGOW BOY 1 See that bunch of jigaboos over there driver?
     Run them over
     You'll be doing us a favour,
     They've taken over.
     If I had a bomb
     That's where I'd drop it.

GLASGOW BOY 2 Why do you live here?

ASYLUM GIRL 1 I have no choice

GLASGOW BOY 2 Why do you have a flat?

ASYLUM GIRL 1 Because Glasgow gave one to us

GLASGOW BOY 2 Why did they give one to *you*?

ASYLUM GIRL 1 Because we have no work. My mother is not allowed to
     work here

GLASGOW BOY 2 But why do they *give* it to you?

ASYLUM GIRL 1 Because we had to leave my country with nothing at all

GLASGOW BOY 2 Why can't you go back home?

ASYLUM GIRL 1 Because they have killed two of my family already
     They would kill us too
     That is why we are asylum seekers

GLASGOW BOY 3 Give us a fag

ASYLUM GIRL 2 I don't smoke

GLASGOW BOY 3 Give us some money

ASYLUM GIRL 2 I have no money

GLASGOW BOY 3 You've all got money

ASYLUM GIRL 2 I've got no money

GLASGOW BOY 3 You've got a flat
     You've got a kitchen
     You've got furniture
     You've got clothes
     You've got a phone
     You've got money

     All you've got is new and you've got everything

ASYLUM GIRL 2 I didn't ask to have all that

GLASGOW BOY 3 I didn't ask you to come here either
                 But since you're here
                 Give us some money

ASYLUM GIRL 2 I've got no money
                 Why don't you understand
                 I've got no money

GLASGOW BOY 3 Give us something or you're not leaving

ASYLUM GIRL 2 I've got a voucher

GLASGOW BOY 3 Fuck your voucher
                 I'm not walking into a shop with a voucher

ASYLUM GIRL 2 That's all I can give you

GLASGOW BOY 3 Give us your phone

ASYLUM GIRL 2 No, it's mine
                 It's to ring the police and that's why I've got it

GLASGOW BOY 3 Go on, see if I care
                 Give us a kiss
                 You've got lips
                 Kiss me

ASYLUM GIRL 2 You asked for it
                 I've got TB I've got AIDS I've got cholera I've got cancer I've
                   got six incurable diseases and you can die from everyone
                 I've got anger I've got homeless disease I've got black skin
                   I've been whipped I've been raped I've been kicked across
                   the world I'm infectious I'm misery I'm death on contact.
                 Kiss me Glasgow boy
                 Kiss me and die.

———————

Dance of the Asylums
Music: 'Blown away like dust' by Robert Moran

While walking back to centre stage and sitting back-to-back:

ALL   I came to Dover in a lorry
I flew to Gatwick in the baggage hold
I came in a little boat on a still night to Somewhere-on-Sea
I came in a cart and a bus and a boat and a truck and a train
And then in a plane

ST MUNGO   Welcome to the United Kingdom

ALL   Where can we stay?

ST MUNGO   Glasgow

ALL   Where is Glasgow?

ST MUNGO   Scotland

ALL   Where is Scotland?

ST MUNGO   North

ALL   Far north?

ST MUNGO   North of north

ALL   Where's that?

ST MUNGO   Castlemilk Pollok Gorbals Springburn Govan Sighthill Royston

ALL   Will we live there?

ST MUNGO   Now you will

ALL   Will we stay?

ST MUNGO   To qualify for membership of Club Asylum you must show
that you have a fear of persecution in your country

ALL   Will we stay?

ST MUNGO   First, you must answer many questions

ALL   Will we stay?

ST MUNGO If your answers are believed, you will.

What is your name?

Age?

What country did you leave?

Why did you leave?

Who did you leave behind?

Walking backwards to upstage:

ALL I left my dog,
My tortoise,
My skates,
My clothes,
My books,
My photos,
My friends,
My house,
My street,
My mother,
My gran and grandad
My aunties and cousins
And my enemies and my town
And the cinema and the park
And the ground and the sky
And the sun and the moon
And the whole world of me is not mine no more

———————

Dance of the Journey
Music: 'Sosu Journey' by Kronos Quartet

ST MUNGO (*During dance.*) I am St Mungo
I sleep so long sometimes
I miss the life of an entire forest

They've planted, grown and cut it down
And still I'm dreaming

When you've lived as long as me
You've outlived even the oldest tree
I'm so old I'm young
No one wakes as fresh as me

I fell asleep about 1950
Sometimes I thought
I heard some shouts to wake me
I always turned over
Drifted off
I slumbered for over half a century
Just like I used to
The morning I awoke
I walked up at dawn onto the Necropolis
And saw coaches leaving London
I heard the far-off sound of mothers crying
Someone south had said my city is a cruel place
Those families cannot prosper here –
Maybe I was dreaming
But the dream was strong
It broke my sleep
My life is long
My roots are deep
What a city I saw as I awoke
Towers surrounding the dear green place
I was like a child
I had to learn to cross the road again

Dance of the Journey continues.

ALL   I live in Glasgow now and I'm not leaving.
       I live in Glasgow now and I'm not leaving.

       I speak ninety-nine languages that nobody wants to learn
       I practise all kinds of religions that get me in all kinds of
         trouble
       I miss home like hell and hell is where my home is

I want to fit into the landscape but I stand out a mile
I want to I want to I want to I want to be like you

I hate my shoes
I hate my foreign name
I hate my foreign face
I hate my stupid English
I hate to have to live in this bloody Scottish place

I learn your language
I take charity
I eat pies
I'm in a play about refugees a lady asked us to do

Movement leading to sitting downstage.

I came to Sighthill with a plastic bag I go to Pinkston
We have a flat two beds a cooker knives forks spoons
A shower a telephone a table chairs towels teabags toilet
   paper
A carpet and hooks on the wall everything new
I hang up my plastic bag on one hook and my clothes on
   another
I lie on the floor and put on the TV
Oh my GAAD this is luxury
Then I go out and some stupid girls spit at me
I spit at them
They spit at me
I go inside my new door
And watch TV
I don't care

All fall back.

I'm Albanian
Kosovan
Rwandan
Colombian
Iranian
Somalian
Pakistani
Afghanistani
Chinese

Congolese
Angolan
Sierra Leonean
Ghanaian
Lithuanian

All sit up.

Algerian
Lebanese
Sudanese

All stand.

Kurdish
Kenyan
Ukrainian
Eritrean
Romanian
Russian
Czech
Indian
Sri Lankan
Yugoslavian
Zimbabwean
Cameroonian
Nigerian

I no speak
I speak no English
I speak little English
I speak English very good
I speak three languages
I speak my language, I speak your language, I speak Glasgee

Movement.

GIRLS   My mother says she's turned into a cow
She counts the clouds that pass our window
She doesn't talk to anyone all day
She no speak English

Pause.

She no speak at all

BOYS My father is a fighting man
He made speeches for the revolution
He is a hero a big guy you say in my country
He was tortured and he never speaks they cannot make him
He is silent in the pain a hero my father
He cannot speak English
He does not try
He is not interested
'Why English?' he say to me, 'why?
I have nothing to say in Sighthill
I am nothing in Scotland'

I'm an asylum
I'm from asylumseekerstan
I'm an asylumseekerstani

GIRLS I'm an asylum
I'm from asylumseekerstan
I'm an asylumseekerstani

————————

ST MUNGO My birth was a miracle.
They expected too much of me.
I could do magic, I had the gift
The salmon, the bell, the bird, the tree
That's all the city knows of me
That, and my last words of course,
I was eighty-five and lying in a bath that was supposed to be
   hot
In which, as you may have read, I caught my death.
'My children, love one another; be hospitable;
Let Glasgow Flourish'
Someone wrote it down.
They've named all sorts of places after me –
Shelters for the homeless
Lifeboats – naturally – any charity or foundation
Where the lost are found
Where refuge, safety, warmth are desperately sought

Where people are treated viciously by others
As helpless as my mother in a cart upon the sea.
They're my work.
I give asylum to those who seek it
I do my best.

It's hard these days

So many questions…

Dance of Freedom
Music: 'Butterfly Dance' by Talvin Singh

ST MUNGO questions *ALL:*

If you claim to have received ill treatment or harassment, who
    was responsible for this treatment?

Why do you believe that this treatment occurred?

Did you report any of the incidents that you have just
    described to the police or to other state authorities?

If not, why not?

If yes, what was their reaction?

Has any of your family received the same or similar
    treatment?

Have you ever moved to a different town or village or to
    another part of your country to avoid the incidents you have
    described above?

If not, why not?

Have you ever been arrested, charged with any offence or
    detained?

Has any member of your family ever been arrested, charged
    with any offence or detained?

Are there any charges outstanding against you or any
    member of your family? If so why?

To which race, ethnic group or nationality do you belong?

What proportion of the population of your home village or
   town is of the same race, ethnic group or nationality as you?

What religious group do you belong to?

Have you always been of this religious faith?

What are the basic beliefs of your religion?

What proportion of the population of your home village or
   town is of the same religion as you?

Do you have any difficulty practising your religion in your
   home country?

Are you a member of any political organization? If so which
   one?

Why, when and where did you become involved with this
   organization?

What type of organization is it, in which part of your country
   is it based and how many members does it have?

For what basic principles does it stand?

What is the nature of your involvement with the organization?

Have you attended any rallies, demonstrations or public
   meetings of the organization?

Have any members of your family been involved with the
   organization?

You are personally responsible for the accuracy of the
   statements contained in this form and the declaration must
   be signed by you.

ALL *hand their forms to* **ST MUNGO**.

He blows them out to the audience.

Dance continues.

ALL   We are waiting
         Did we give the right answer
         Or the wrong answer?

Are we in Club Asylum
Or are we out?
Are we refugees
Or are we deportees?
We are waiting
We are waiting
We are waiting

Club Asylum Dance: 'Asian Warrior', 'Mad Mungo', 'The Twins from Siam', 'King Kurd'

At the end of the dance:

ALL We are waiting
We are waiting
We are waiting

ST MUNGO What is asylum?
Asylum is safety
Safety from what?
Safety from home

What's an asylum?
What's an asylum seeker?
What's an asylum seeker seek
When an asylum seeker's seeking?

———————

ALL bring out chairs and sit.

TEACHER I've got a third-year PSD class and that was the first
opportunity there was for anyone to bring up the events of
September the Eleventh. It's a very mixed class in terms of
religion, in terms of colour, unusually so for Glasgow, and
we had a chat about it and everyone said how horrified
they'd been… Now there is one boy in that class from the
Middle East who said –

'Well it's not nice but I don't get as shocked as easily as
   that – '
Someone said 'Why not?'
He was able then to say,
'Well, you know I saw my family killed in front of me
I've seen houses burned, businesses burned, animals
   burned, children shot, people tortured'
And the class went absolutely silent
And they all listened
And they all looked ashen-faced
And for the first time I think they were actually associating
   just what it was to be one of these asylum seeking children.
He had now the courage to speak a little bit about it,
He didn't need to go into any detail,
He simply alluded to it
For a minute the whole class, without exception, saw his
   situation
With absolute clarity

FASCIST Asylum?
Place for loonies

Asylum seekers?
Trash – murderers, rapists, thieves, you don't know do you?

They're running, says it all, easy

I know what they're running to
Free flat free school free phone
Free food on your fucking plate four times a day
Easy

They come from another world
Their world their problem
I'd take them up to the top floor
And show them my world
Then kick 'em off one by one

Splat, splat, splat, splat, splat, splat
Easy

No, Glasgow must say no
No, no, no

YOUNG ASIAN GUY

Asylum's a place with some level of safety
Some level of democracy

Asylum seekers are usually escaping a political regime
That dictates to them how they should actually live

They've come to a land of hope
A place where they might find happiness
They've left behind their land of origin
Where the air is the air breathed from the hour you were born
Memories, water, friends, land, language
They've left all that behind
That's how I arrived nine years ago.
To a place where language
Where climate are so completely different

Where I live near Pollokshields
It's asylum heaven
I see kids smiling
Free to go about
Families walking together
That's a good thing

I know how Glasgow operates
Asylum seekers bring whole lives with them
Asylum seekers bring whole worlds
That is what causes friction
Asylums live with fear
I know

Since the Eleventh of September, they take me for one

MARTIAL ARTS TEACHER

Ignorance is armed –
It carries knives and
It uses them on people it doesn't understand

I teach self-defence on Tuesdays to asylums
I started in May 2000 with five
Now I get a minimum thirty every week and it's growing
I love them, it's simple as that,

That's why I do it voluntarily.
It was total chaos in the first part of 2000
In fact most of that year
No one was consulted
No one was ready
The schools and the police just had to catch up
There were no translators no organization
No attempt to inform the residents of our estate

The asylums were in mortal danger
And they didn't even know it
They thought they were in a civilized country
It was scandalous, no question about it
I think that the council's catching up now
With the sheer scale of what it's done.

I'm part of that
In my way

Everyone has the right to self-defence.

FASCIST   I want to show you something
Maybe you've seen it
I put it up two days after September the Eleventh

'All Asians be careful.
I have spent last night witnessing what you did.
There is no way you can live in my country any longer.
I am warning you to leave now.
This is racial hatred not out of ignorance.
You are a threat to me.
If you remain here you will die.'

I'll do it alone
I have no fear of trash
Bring them on friend
In fives and tens
Watch the city burn
Watch the river burn
Easy

YOUNG ASIAN GUY

> This first bunch of asylum seekers
> Are pioneers
> In the front line overnight
> It's very hard for them now
> Very hard
> But it will make them strong
>
> In ten years they'll be getting good jobs
> All over
> You'll see

TEACHER So then I asked the children
> Where would you seek asylum
> If you had to leave Glasgow suddenly
> And you could never come back?
> If you could never come back
> Because a terrorist had crashed a plane into a nuclear power
>   station
> And the whole country was radioactive
> Several said Spain…
> When they realised England was too close
> Quite a few chose Florida
> I said it's not a holiday
> You have to go there and stay for ever and never come home
>   again
> And you've only time to pack a carrier bag
> Where would you go?
> Some said Australia…
> And then I told them about the asylum seekers there,
> The ones who sewed up their mouths in protest
> At having to wait so long for a decision
>
> At the end of the lesson I asked them where Kosovo is.
> Most of them placed it on the other side of the world
> One boy knew but that was the same child who'd spoken
>   earlier.
> They were interested to discover it's two hours away.
> The next day two mothers phoned the head
> To complain that their kids had had nightmares

I promised to keep politics out of school.
I've had to.

MARTIAL ARTS TEACHER
I've made friends with quite a few of my students
One of them is called Najma.
She's Somalian and she lives two floors up.
She's a single mum with two gorgeous boys,
Twins, both seventeen.
They've learnt to speak English better and better
Over the last year and we've grown closer.
We cook meals for each other.
And my own lad is learning.
He goes out anywhere he wants with the twins,
He's lost that fear in twelve months.
Najma assists me now on Tuesdays
And an Estonian and a Ghanaian help her.
I've got a small army of translators to help.
Sometimes I feel Glasgow council is planting a new city
In the dying parts of the old one.

Song: 'Mother Glasgow' by Michael Marra

ALL (*Sing.*) In the second city of the empire
Mother Glasgow watches all her wains
Trying hard to feed her little starlings
Unconsciously she clips their little wings

Mother Glasgow's succour is perpetual
Nestling the Billy and the Tim
I dreamt I took a dander with St Mungo
To try to catch a fish that couldna' swim

Among the flightless birds and sightless starlings
Father Glasgow knows his starlings well
He won't make his own way up to heaven
By waltzing all his charges into hell

Mother Glasgow's succour is perpetual
Nestling the Billy and the Tim
I dreamt I took a dander with St Mungo
To try to catch a fish that couldna' swim

And the tree and the fish and the bird and the bell

Let Glasgow flourish

———————

ST MUNGO First
It was easy
We made a home here
Around my church
The fishermen
Made a village
The travellers
A port
The traders
A town
The merchants
A city
For a thousand years
Or more
It grew

I worked in many places
Far from home
The dear green place
I left alone

(Then they came)

The Highlanders had their homes taken from them
Nowhere to live nothing to eat

(They came to Glasgow)

The Irish had nothing, no homes and no food

(They came to Glasgow)

Four million Jews persecuted in Russia

(Jews came to Glasgow)

The Nazis killed six million Poles

(Poles came to Glasgow)

Italians so poor

(Some walked to Glasgow)

Revolution in China

(More came to Glasgow)

In India, Pakistan, Bangladesh, everything
Poverty
Famine
Massacre
Misrule

(They came to Glasgow)

Most Glaswegians come from somewhere else

Even St Mungo

Aftermath of Murder of Firsit Dag
(*This is a direct quotation from a newspaper. Davoud Rasal
Naseri was slashed outside his flat in Sighthill on 7 August
2001. Firsit Dag was murdered on his way home to Sighthill
in the early hours of 5 August 2001.*)

DAVOUD RASAL NASERI
(*Through an interpreter.*)
My name is Davoud Rasal Naseri. Today is the twentieth of
August 2001.
I was putting my rubbish out.
The three men attacked me from behind.
And suddenly one slashed with a knife.

Is this really any better than Iran?

At first I was very happy that I was in a safe country and
could live in comfort and safety.

But it didn't last too long.

Regarding what is going on recently I don't feel safe any
longer.

I just feel that I hate Glasgow and I hate the people in
Glasgow.

With this recent situation, I just want to stay in my country, it
would be better for me because I would be killed because of
my aims, not because of nothing.

I never thought it was going to be this way before coming
here.

The idea I got was that UK had very good people, very
hospitable people, but now my idea regarding the people
has completely changed.

I am not going to think in this way anymore.

I am now frightened of Glasgow and I do not want to
continue living here.

I want to seek asylum from Glasgow.

I want to seek asylum from Glasgow.

ALL gather around him.

ASYLUM SEEKERS   What is asylum?
Asylum is safety

When we ran from my country
We were refugees
When we arrive in your country
We are not refugees
We are asylum seekers

We ask you to believe us
That we are refugees
We were blown away
We are dust

We are telling you as strongly and as firmly as we can
We are dust
We assert

We are dust
We insist
We are dust
We swear
We are dust
If you blow on us
We disappear

_____

ST MUNGO Kosovo Kosova
Iraq Iran
Turkish Kurdish
Christian Muslim
Catholic Protestant
Rich poor
Famine plenty
Man woman
Old Labour New Labour
Scotland England
Edinburgh Glasgow
One in one out

Those who know who asylum seekers are
Don't attack them

Those who attack them
Don't know who asylum seekers are

_____

ASYLUM SEEKERS Who am I?
Why do I have to ask?
You know who you are.
You've never had to ask yourself.
I never had to ask myself.
When my home really was my home.

When my home was in my country.
When my home wasn't in your home.
When my flat wasn't next to your flat.
When I lived in a city that knew as little about your city
As you in your city know about my city
Who am I?
I used to know the answer because I didn't have to ask the
  question.
The same way you don't have to ask
Who am I?

I'm an asylum seeker.
I seek asylum from my home in your home.
My old home is no longer home.
My old home is burnt down on a battlefield.
And all the other homes around my home got burnt down in
  the battle.
I'm an asylum seeker.
I'm a home seeker.
I will take a home from anyone who has a home to give.
I live anywhere I'm told.
Because anywhere in your country is better
Than everywhere in my country.
Who am I?
That I'm so happy to be where no one else is happy to be.
Who am I?
That thinks Glasgow is the best place in the world for me.
Who am I?
That sees how much you've got, not how little.

I've lived here a while
I've never lived anywhere like this in my life before
The language, the lifts, the winter.
If you went and lived in my home
You would feel as lost as I do
You would wonder all the time
Who you are
You would look a total stranger
With your beggar family asking for shelter
You would have no friends, no jokes, no faith, no courage
You would love anyone in my home who was kind to you

Who made you feel
Who you are and not have to ask,
Who am I?

Most people in Glasgow are kind
The policemen, the teachers, the spokesmen,
The man who fixed the washing machine
And said we were welcome in his country
And asked us to his home the week we arrived.
The priest who is not of our religion
Who asked us to come to his church party
The crazy boy who threw stones at my sister in the road
Whose dad brought him round to apologise
And he cried when he looked at the cut on her face
The lady who organised a trip to Edinburgh Castle in July
These people say you are who you are
You stop wondering and you stop asking
Who am I?

Let me stay in Sighthill
The best place in the world
The best place in the world
Prince William is on my wall
Prince William is walking up to me and my friends
He's shaking my hand
He's smiling
Do you know how amazing he is
When you don't know exactly the answer
To the bloody question
Who am I?

Maybe it's true
I am who I am
Today is a new day
I speak a new language now
I wear a shirt and a tie to school
I'm making sense of what teachers say to me
And the headmaster says
There are no asylum seekers
Just new Glaswegians and old Glaswegians
Maybe it's not true

Maybe it will be
I'm a new language new uniform new face new braveheart
  Glaswegian
I'm beginning to know who I am again
I'm no longer thinking
Who am I?
As long as I can stay
Just as long as I can stay
Some of my friends have leave to remain
Some of my friends are refugees
But I don't know yet. But I don't know yet.
What if they tell me I'm no longer a new Glaswegian
And my family is not welcome
And my home is not here
And I'm going back on a plane on Sunday
Goodbye school, weather, lifts
Goodbye the plumber the priest the lady the father
Goodbye my lovely teacher
Who once was an asylum seeker himself
Goodbye Glasgow
Into the night and a plane
Then I will know who I am
I will be an asylum seeker
All my damned life
So every night I pray
Every night I pray

Let me stay in Glasgow
Let me stay at my school
Let me stay in my flat
Let me stay home

Can't say goodbye
Blown away again
Middle of the night again
Back of a truck again
Not knowing what will become of us
Asylum seekers seeking somewhere to seek asylum

VIRGINS

for Hanna and Jack

Background

I read an academic paper that says English and American families tend to dramatise adolescent sexuality (highlight negative risks and speak ominously about the consequences – pregnancy, infection, effect of drugs, etc). Dutch and Scandinavian families, on the other hand, tend to normalise it; that is, they talk openly about their sexual lives, accommodate the changes and see little cause for over-reaction. After all, parents have been there before, haven't they?

The drama of *Virgins* springs (naturally) from a family that dramatises sexuality rather than normalising it. Jack's night at the party is his own 'dramatic' response. A 'Dutch family' would have talked through the pointlessness of a night like that long ago. Jack's family are reactive and unable to open up the subject until it has become an actual source of conflict.

A key aspect is the sexuality of the parents themselves. Adolescents have a natural urge to place their own dramas centre-stage – but if the family is a happy one there will be a sexual narrative going on with the parents as well. At certain points in a family's life, there is a great deal of discrete sexual energy under one roof. English houses are quite small and all the bedrooms are usually on the same floor. To normalise everything as effectively as the Northern Europeans do requires a more sexually enlightened culture than the one I know.

Here are a couple of interesting quotes that we put in the programme for *Virgins*:

> The present controversies about family values – about marriage and the divorce rate – are really discussions about monogamy, about what keeps people together and why they should stay together. […] What are couples for if they are not for pleasure? And if pleasure does not matter, then what does?
>
> (From *Monogamy* by Adam Phillips (Faber 1996))

> Children are expected to retain a sexual naivety and to be passive onlookers on a highly sexualised culture […] But for all that teenagers are over-informed about how other people do it, this has not brought young men and women any closer to developing an erotic language […] In a world where I often feel every experience has been flayed of flavour through over-exposure, sex is one of the few things that retain its tang […] But until adults can address the double standard that surrounds young people's experience of intimacy, this will remain a sexual revolution in waiting […] If we are to reach a consensus on the kinds of moral ambitions and characters we want our children to have, then we

need to return to a notion of common citizenship. Parenting cannot happen in isolation. Children themselves can play an active part in their own development.

(From *The Story of Childhood – Growing up in Modern Britain*
by Libby Brooks (Bloomsbury 2006))

Characters

NICK, Dad, about 40

SUZY, Mum, about 40

JACK, Son, 17

ZOE, Daughter, 15

All four are on stage, sitting at the side when not in a scene.

PLACE: A terraced, three-bedroom house and a nearby wood in the South of England.

TIME: The action takes place over six Sundays in the present day.

SET: A dance space, with reflective dance floor and light panels behind, bare but for a scale model 'Barratts' home, large enough for one family member to get inside, which can be freely pushed around the floor, and three multi-purpose boxes distributed around the space.

MUSIC: 'John's Book of Alleged Dances' by John Adams (performed by Kronos Quartet); Bach's 'Viola de Gamba' Sonatas (performed by Pieter Wispelwey); 'Certain Romance' by the Arctic Monkeys.

TELEPHONE CALLS: Sadie, Beth, Ben and other callers are pre-recorded voices.

DANCE: The play is about a family who live together under one roof in a terraced three-bedroom house. Despite individual tensions, each member has an urge to keep the family together. Yet they often reach a point where they cannot say what they want to say to each other. What they cannot articulate, they say through dance.

Dance will focus on the relationships within the family – but it is not always illustrative of the action at the moment the dance begins.

Virgins was first performed at the Junction Theatre, Cambridge, on 28 July 2006 with the following company:

JACK, Stefan Butler
SUZY, Becky Fortune
NICK, Peter Machen
ZOE, Emily Woodward

Director John Retallack
Choreographer Fleur Darkin
Designer Liz Cooke
Lighting Designer Mark Dymock
Sound Designer Daniel Alcock
Set Builder Rupert Blakeley at Oxford Theatre Workshops

Virgins was a Company of Angels production in association with The Junction, Cambridge. It was subsequently performed at the Edinburgh Festival (5–28 August 2006) and toured England in September and October 2006.

Virgins was commissioned through an Arts Council England grant. The Soho Theatre and Lyric Theatre, Hammersmith, and the PULSE Festival, Ipswich, gave support in the development of the play through public readings. The Centre Départemental de Résidence d'Ecrivains Européens of Villa Mont-Noir near Lille, France, enabled the first draft of *Virgins* to be written in late 2004. The production was supported by Arts Council England. Arts Council England East made it possible to bring *Virgins* to the Edinburgh Festival through an East to Edinburgh grant.

Scene One

FIRST SUNDAY

JACK and ZOE are sleeping.

Nick & Suzy Bedroom Exchange (1)

Each one of these four exchanges has a different choreographic shape.

NICK Please turn over and look at me

SUZY No

NICK I'm sorry about what I said

SUZY No Nick

NICK Please turn over

SUZY No

NICK Please

SUZY I don't want to

NICK Suzy!

SUZY I want to sleep

NICK Sleep this way

SUZY No

NICK Why not?

SUZY You know why

NICK Why?

SUZY You'll start again

NICK What's wrong with that?

SUZY I don't want to Nick, doesn't that matter to you?

NICK Maybe if you turn over I'll change your mind

SUZY You won't

NICK Had enough?

SUZY Yes

NICK Had enough of me? Is that it?

SUZY I just want to sleep

NICK Then go to sleep

SUZY Nothing will stop me

NICK Great – I'll go and run myself a cold bath

SUZY You do what you like, just let me sleep – and please don't wake the children.

NICK Nothing wakes the children

SUZY Shut the door quietly.

SECOND SUNDAY

ZOE I'm writing my diary for the week while it's calm
Mum and Dad aren't up yet
I fed the cat
Jack is asleep
And because he forgets to turn his alarm off at weekends
It went off at seven
It went off very loud
Right next to his ear
I'm the one who has to go and stop it

He's lying there fully dressed
With the sun full in his face.
His clothes and his hair stink of smoke and drink –
He's only been back a short time.
I was at the same party
And I left it a whole day earlier

He's alive
Just dead till the afternoon

I like it when everyone's asleep
The quiet is different to other quiet
It's Sunday quiet

JACK I'm trying to behave as normally as I can
So that Mum and Dad won't ask too many questions
When they get up

It's Sunday and I'm home

Right now I am on a totally different planet to everyone else

I woke up in the front garden at six
I don't know how I got there
I got to my bed without disturbing the snores from their room.

When I woke up
I never felt so bad in my life
My heart was really pounding
I thought I'd faint
Then I felt so sick
I couldn't stand I was so dizzy

I'm up now and I'm practising being normal
But I'm not normal
Not anymore

Last night is a complete blank
Except for one thing
I had sex
I had sex with Sadie Bennett on the floor of the bathroom at
  the party
Sadie Bennett
I had sex with Sadie Bennett

I've always fancied her
And she was there!
I was away, I was flying, I mean I was totally out my skin
And we danced and she laughed at everything I said
And she was well gone too
And I just knew it was on
At last
I knew it

And then what?

Oh God…

What happened after?

What the hell happened next?

He picks up his phone and calls Ben.

ZOE   I met a boy at the party.
      He's got manners
      He's incredibly polite;
      He's tall and thin with deep brown eyes
      He's been in England for two years

His parents are dead
He told me
That's why he's here,
His uncle and aunt live in Southside.
He came to the party but it's not his scene
When you see it through his eyes
You can see why it's not.
He doesn't drink for a start and drugs just aren't on his list.
He's got self-control,
Not like Jack and his mob.
They *stampede* the girls,
They're in such a rush
They don't know what they're doing
This boy – he's beyond all that.
He's calm; he's not hurried,
He's not thirsty all the time like the rest of them
He doesn't smoke either.
He has a sweet scent about him.
I can't work out what it is –
I want to know
I want to buy it and wear it on *me*.
Calm, calm.
It'll take time.
If he is to trust me
I will have to be patient and calm too
I want to know him better,
Much better than I do now,
I've been thinking about him all night.
I don't know his name.
He kissed me goodbye.

Gestures.

Just here.
That was so *nice.*

Nick & Suzy Bedroom Exchange (2)

NICK Hullo babe, how are you?

SUZY Sleepy, let me sleep a bit more

NICK Oh come on Suzy…it's Sunday morning

SUZY   What time is it?

NICK   Half past eight – the children won't be awake for ages yet

       He kisses her.

SUZY   Oh don't, I haven't even cleaned my teeth

       Pause.

NICK   Go on then

SUZY   I'm going Nick, I'm just very comfortable right now

       *Sigh from **NICK**.*

       I'm going Nick; you're a bit pushy aren't you?

NICK   I'm sorry – I've been awake since six

SUZY   You drink too much, that's why Nick

NICK   Jack woke me coming in.

SUZY   Wine makes you grumpy in the mornings

NICK   I am not grumpy. Except with Jack. You're grumpy.

SUZY   I was asleep Nick

NICK   You said you had to start at nine and it's now half past eight
       on Sunday morning…

SUZY   So it is…

       He kisses her again.

       Nick don't – please don't start again – I am tired – you just
       don't understand what work means anymore do you?
       – Sunday is my only day of rest and I want to *sleep*! When
       else am I meant to catch up? Get off me Nick – I want to be
       safe in my own bed! Not mauled!

       Beat.

NICK   (*Quietly.*) Alright

THIRD SUNDAY

       Music.

ZOE   I've had my phone on vibrate
       Ever since the morning after the party
       It's in my pocket ALL THE TIME

Even when I'm asleep
I am on total alert
And he hasn't called yet.
I always check in case I missed a call.
It goes off loads.
But it's always Sophie
It's never him.

JACK   (*On phone.*) Hi Ben
I been trying to get you
I'm pissing razors man. It's agony.
You ever had anything like that?

BEN   (*On phone.*) I'm clean
What've you got?

JACK   Could be gonorrhoea

BEN   That's harsh

JACK   Or even herpes...or syphilis – I can't believe it.
I checked out the internet –
I seem to have the symptoms of everything.
It's so nasty
I feel so dirty

BEN   You should go to the clinic – see a nurse

JACK   Oh man...

BEN   Careful you don't get a biggy – in front of her, like

JACK   Whatever

BEN   It happens
Happened to Craig.

JACK   Sadie gave me it

BEN   Not her Jack

JACK   Who else then!?

BEN   Don't you remember what happened?

JACK   What?

BEN   I'm looking at it on my phone now

JACK   What?

BEN   You and Beth Green

JACK Beth Green!?

BEN You had sex in the back seat of Carol's dad's Skoda which was parked at the side of the house

JACK I can't – that never happened – I – I remember nothing

BEN Listen up Jack – you don't remember anything because you were so far off your face on everything, you didn't know what you were doing! You were an animal Jack!

JACK Me – ? I – ? It's a total blank mate

BEN You were gettin' on Beth in the car with a whole crowd of us round the windows trying to stop you – but you locked the doors!

JACK But what about Beth?

BEN She was as far off her face as you man – she is such a skunk – you know that – God knows what you picked up from her man – you're not really telling me you don't remember – do you want the picture?

JACK No – please delete it man

BEN Alright – coming up – you sure you don't want to see?

JACK Sure. Thanks Ben.

BEN It's done man. You'll be alright. Just lay low for a bit. Go and see nursey. It'll blow over.

JACK Okay

BEN Later on yeah

JACK I still can't believe it

BEN You better believe it! I did everything I could to stop you but…you were beyond beyond, Jack.

JACK Jesus. I don't know. Okay. Later on…

BEN Take my advice – lie low.

JACK *closes the phone and doesn't move.*

Nick & Suzy Bedroom Exchange (3)

NICK You looked at your watch

SUZY What?

NICK   We are making love and you just looked at your watch

SUZY   Nick, you're imagining things

NICK   No I'm not – you've a lot to do on your day of rest and making love to me has to be done by 9 AM!

SUZY   Nick…

NICK   It does, doesn't it?

SUZY   No Nick

NICK   I'm actually in you and you are looking at the fucking time!

SUZY   Don't you dare swear at me!

NICK   I'll swear all I want!

SUZY   Then get off me!

NICK   Oh go on, get up and get to work!

SUZY   I will

NICK   (*Louder.*) You looked at your watch in the middle of sex – Sunday is the only time of the week you admit that you're relaxed enough and not too exhausted to have intercourse with your husband –

SUZY   (*Hisses.*) Nick, you'll wake Jack and Zoe – you did that last week, Zoe actually asked me what you were shouting about – keep your voice down or I will walk out of the door and you won't see me for a week!

NICK   (*Hisses back.*) I won't see you for a week anyway! Just what is the difference? You're just not really there anymore are you? The only thing that turns you on in this world is your fucking job!

SUZY   Calm down Nick! Don't talk like this! You'll destroy any feeling between us if you carry on.

        Beat.

NICK   You don't love me

SUZY   I do love you

NICK   But?

SUZY   We need time together. That's all

NICK   And until we do 'have time'?

SUZY I don't know.

Beat. **NICK** *sighs.*

Hold me Nick, just hold me. That's something we can do now

NICK Oh for God's sake!

SUZY How can you call me cold, you won't hold me unless we have sex; it's you that's cold, not me!

NICK Oh it's nine o'clock, time's up…

SUZY Stop moaning Nick – that's never going to turn me on – in fact it turns me off more than anything else about you

FOURTH SUNDAY

Music.

ZOE What are you doing up so early?

JACK I can't sleep

ZOE I didn't hear you come in

JACK I didn't go out

ZOE What were you doing?

JACK Stayed in my room

ZOE On Saturday night?

JACK Yes

ZOE Is there something wrong with you?

JACK Yeah there is

ZOE What kind of thing?

JACK You won't tell anyone?

ZOE Why are you telling me?

JACK Who else can I talk to Zo?

ZOE Ben?

JACK No I can't

ZOE Or Craig?

JACK No

ZOE Daniel?

JACK shakes his head. He shudders.

Tell me

JACK Promise you won't tell?

ZOE Promise

Nick & Suzy Bedroom Exchange (4)

NICK That's better. You smell nice

SUZY I don't feel very nice

NICK I'll make you feel nice

SUZY Will you, Nick?

NICK Don't sound so doubtful

SUZY I'm not…it's just been a long week

NICK Of course

SUZY Including all Saturday

NICK And so will next week be a long week

SUZY You know I can't help that

NICK I know I know

SUZY Just stroke me Nick please

NICK Alright

SUZY My back

NICK Last week I stroked you and you fell back to sleep

SUZY Did I?

NICK Yes

SUZY I won't today Nick I promise

Silence as he strokes.

That's nice

He continues.

NICK It's like stroking a dead body

SUZY That's it, I'm getting up.

Dance of the Family: Suzy, Nick, Jack, Zoe
Music: Adams or Bach

This is four individuals pulling in four different directions who each aspire to be part of a cohesive and loyal unit called a family.

Dance segues to:

Scene Two

FIFTH SUNDAY

JACK What! You told Dad!?

ZOE Yes

JACK Why?

ZOE Because you won't tell anyone

JACK I told you

ZOE But you don't listen to me Jack!
Anyway, Dad really understands
He said he was young too.

JACK You told him everything?

ZOE I had to

JACK He'll go nuts!

ZOE He'll be fine

Enter NICK.

NICK Zoe says you haven't been to the doctor yet?

JACK (*Shocked.*) I'm going tomorrow

NICK You should have gone there by now, right?

JACK Yes Dad

NICK Have you considered that one of the girls might be pregnant too?

Beat.

JACK Of course I have –

NICK Of course you haven't.

ZOE Don't get stressed Dad, you said you wouldn't!

NICK (*To ZOE.*) If Jack has made a girl pregnant, then Jack is responsible.

As a seventeen year-old father it will be *his* duty to look after both mother and child.

ZOE Dad, you said you would *discuss* it with him.

NICK Jack should know a few things, that's all.

Beat.

JACK I'd be eighteen

NICK What?

JACK I'll be eighteen if she had a baby, not seventeen, Dad; it's nine months.

NICK Don't try and be funny Jack.

Goodbye uni, goodbye future, goodbye freedom…

JACK Yes Dad

ZOE You promised you'd help him Dad!

NICK Do you hear me Jack?

JACK I know Dad. I know now.

NICK But you should know better – shouldn't you?

Then you wouldn't be in this mess.

JACK Alright Dad. Thanks Dad.

Beat.

NICK Don't try to stop me talking about it.

JACK It's just you never talked about it before Dad…

NICK Oh so is this my fault?

JACK No it's not your fault, Dad.

NICK And now it's all happening, you don't want to talk about it?

You just want to go round sticking it in when and where you like, as and when you feel like it – is that it?

JACK's phone goes off loudly in his pocket.

It's impossible to talk to you for five minutes without that going off!

JACK (*Into phone.*) Jack speaking?

> While **JACK** is on phone, the following between **ZOE** and **NICK** at the same time:

ZOE Dad, this is definitely not what Jack needs

NICK Zoe excuse me but I think I know what I'm doing

ZOE He's upset enough as it is

NICK He doesn't seem upset in the slightest bit

ZOE That's just Jack, you should know that Dad

NICK He needs to be taught a lesson

TARA (*On phone.*) Jack, this is Tara

JACK Hello I can't talk now I'm sorry

TARA You can't talk to me?

JACK I can call you back in an hour, how's that?

TARA Don't forget.

JACK Call back later then – bye.

TARA Bye

NICK Who was that?

JACK Just a friend

NICK What friend?

JACK Tara

NICK Who's Tara?

JACK No one – just one of the group

NICK One of your friends from the party?

JACK I don't know Dad, I don't remember

NICK What do you mean you don't *remember*?

JACK I can't remember…

NICK How can you not remember having sex with someone?

JACK (*Looking at ZOE, panicking a little.*) Dad, I took some drugs. Leave it – I know I was wrong –

NICK (*Can't stop.*) You go out to a neighbour's house – in two hours you get so stoned –

JACK's phone goes off in his pocket.

(*Sotto voce.*) Bloody bloody phones…

NICK starts to fume.

ZOE Turn it off Jack!

JACK takes the call.

JACK (*On phone.*) Jack speaking

YOUNG FEMALE (*On phone.*) Are you coming to the pub?

JACK Can't talk now sweetheart

JACK snaps phone shut.

NICK Who – ?

JACK Just a friend.

NICK stares at him and shakes his head.

JACK Wants me to play pool – it can wait Dad – look – here I am – I'm listening.

Pause.

You said I can use the car tonight…

ZOE Oh Jack…

NICK surveys JACK long enough to make him uncomfortable.

NICK Look at you; you're a mess,

ZOE Dad, stop…

NICK And your room is a rubbish heap and you don't go to bed at night and you never get up in the morning on top of which you spend the money we give you on drugs. Now I find you don't even know who you've had sex with…

JACK We can talk about it Dad

ZOE (*Pulling at NICK.*) There's no need to get so angry.

NICK (*Louder, pulling away.*) You are a waste of time and a waste of space
My father would have beaten the shit out of me if I'd been like you –
You're lucky I've not taken after him aren't you Jack?

JACK's phone goes off again.

NICK explodes.

ZOE Oh my God – I told you to turn it off!

JACK I thought I had!

NICK Give it me! You heard! Give it me!

JACK What are you going to do with it?

NICK Never mind! Give it me!

NICK snatches at the phone.

JACK Dad! That's my phone!

JACK cancels the call.

Look it's off Dad!

NICK grips the phone still in JACK's hand. Both have it in their grip and neither will let it go.

It's my phone!

NICK Paid for with my money –

JACK You gave it to me –

NICK I'm taking it back –

JACK It's not yours to take back –

NICK Let go!

JACK It's mine! Fuck off Dad!

Beat.

NICK Don't fuck off *me*, you little fucker! Let go –

JACK gets the phone away from NICK. NICK launches himself at him and grabs him by the shirt. JACK cannot move and NICK explodes an inch from his face.

SUZY enters – what she sees roots her to the spot.

You careless little shite – do you know what all this means to us, to this family – I don't want you in the same bathroom as me – I don't want you touching the same towel and using the same soap – you've got a sexual infection and you haven't seen a doctor – you are seventeen and you are a *fucking* disaster – you hear that, Jack?

JACK   Yes

NICK   You lose things don't you? You've always lost your bag, your money, your phone – well now you've lost my respect.

NICK shakes him hard at the shoulders.

JACK is really shaken and drops his head.

You make me sick. You *infect* our home. Go on – fend for yourself – get out of it! Out!

*NICK finishes by contemptuously releasing **JACK** and turns to find himself face to face with **SUZY**.*

SUZY   What's going on?

*SUZY goes straight to **JACK** and puts her arm around him.*

What is going on Nick?

NICK   We were having a reasonable discussion together about a recent party Jack went to where he appears to have behaved very stupidly – then his phone kept ringing, I objected and Jack tells me to 'fuck off' – at which point I lost it completely I'm afraid. Sorry.

SUZY   Jack doesn't usually swear at us

NICK   Whatever happens with Jack, you take his side – *that's* why he has no respect towards others. He's just had sex with a complete stranger – and he can't remember anything about it!

SUZY   I want to know what happened, now come on Jack.

JACK   What do you want me to say?

SUZY   I want you to tell me what happened!

*JACK looks at **ZOE**: 'did you really get me into this?'*

*During his 'statement' to **SUZY**, he frequently looks at **ZOE**.*

JACK   I went to a big party three weeks ago.

SUZY   And?

JACK   I had a couple of lines on the way to their place.

SUZY   Sorry, a couple of lines of what?

JACK   Coke, Mum. Cocaine.

SUZY   Oh. And then what?

JACK   I danced with Sadie and we had sex in a room upstairs and though I had a condom with me I forgot to use it. Craig gave me a pill and Ben opened a bottle of vodka and we smoked. I can't remember anything else after that. Not till I woke up on the Sunday morning in the front garden.

SUZY   I think you're lucky to be alive Jack

JACK   Other people do much more than me Mum

SUZY   Is that all you can say?

JACK   Ben told me he saw me having sex with another girl during the party.

SUZY   Did you?

JACK   What?

SUZY   Have sex with this other girl!

JACK   That's it. I can't remember anything about it, nothing at all – I've never spoken to her.

SUZY   What's her name?

JACK   Beth.

SUZY   Beth what?

JACK   Beth Green, what does it matter?

SUZY   So you didn't?

JACK   (*Exasperated.*) I can't say Mum. The thing is I've forgotten more than I remember!

SUZY   Is that it?

JACK   What more do you want?

       *SUZY looks to **NICK**.*

NICK   See? See what we're dealing with?

       *SUZY ignores **NICK** and turns back to **JACK**.*

SUZY   When was the party?

JACK   Three weeks ago

SUZY   Ben is someone that you trust isn't he?

JACK   Trust? Yeah, I trust him; more than anyone else

NICK   You should try meeting new people

JACK   It's not so easy Dad

SUZY   Can we just focus on Jack?

JACK   We were on a binge that night. It was stupid. I know that.

NICK   Oh he knows that now.

SUZY   (*Assertive*.) I want to hear Jack speak. About the party. He
        was there. You weren't. Sadie or Beth may be pregnant…

NICK   Or they both are…

SUZY   (*To **NICK**.*) It's unlikely – but it's possible… We can sort it out!
        No one's dead. Let Jack speak.

        SUZY *looks to* **JACK**.

JACK   (*Shrugs.*) I got nothing else to say

        Beat.

SUZY   If Sadie had an infection then she has infected you.
        So you could have infected the other girl, Beth.

JACK   But Mum, I'm not sure –

SUZY   Or you might have been infected before the party.
        You might have infected Sadie and Beth yourself

JACK   Mum, I definitely know I wasn't infected.

SUZY   Is it a rash or is it a swelling?

JACK   Mum, I'm not discussing it with you, right!

SUZY   Is it on your penis?

JACK   (*Angry.*) I am not discussing it anymore!

NICK   You are talking to your mother –

JACK   Or with you!

SUZY   You must see the doctor, Jack

JACK   I'll decide when I go to a bloody doctor! It's my body, it's
        my life, I am not an extension of you or you, I am an
        independent – human – being – with a will of my own
        – and a life. (*To **NICK**.*) Unlike you!

NICK   (*To **SUZY**.*) Oh just let him go out and screw someone else

SUZY   Oh shut up Nick! You're so crass.

JACK   Oh just have your own stupid arguments! Again…

*Angry and upset, **JACK** walks to the exit.*

SUZY   (*Stops him.*) You *must* see the doctor.
You *have* to talk to the girls

*JACK's phone goes off in **NICK**'s hand. **JACK** freezes. He'd forgotten it.*

JACK   Dad!

NICK   (*Answers phone.*) Hullo – Jack is not available right now

JACK   Give it me!

NICK   Can you ring back in an hour?

*JACK tries to take the phone from **NICK**. **SUZY** holds **JACK** back.*

SUZY   You can't do that Nick, let him have his phone back –

NICK   Thank you – goodbye –

NICK snaps the phone shut.

(*To **SUZY**.*) It never stops.

SUZY   Just ask him to turn it off

NICK   He refuses.

SUZY   Give it to me

NICK   He shouldn't be allowed out Suzy –

SUZY   Give it to me Nick or I am going to get so angry

NICK   Take it – I don't want it

*NICK gives it to **SUZY**. **SUZY** gives it to **JACK**.*

SUZY   Where are you going Jack?

JACK   Out!

SUZY   Please don't go, we can all talk about this calmly, I'm sure we
can

JACK   I'm not talking to Dad again, not EVER!

NICK   You don't have to, just GO!

*JACK exits, **ZOE** follows him to exit.*

ZOE remains listening to her parents talk; they don't see her.

SUZY   Are you trying to drive your son out of the house for good?

NICK   Yes! It's time he went! He's a fucking pest!

SUZY Too much for you, is he?

NICK Yes, he is. I live with him; you don't.

SUZY I do

NICK Oh? *What* do you do? I get him up, I get his breakfast, I make him do his homework, I wash his clothes, I write his frequent letters of absence, I lend him money I don't get back, I stay awake in bed until he comes home and fret if he's been knifed or mugged. But what's he doing all that time? Drink, drugs and random sex. The boy's an animal. He'll follow his prick anywhere. Sure I want him out.

Beat.

SUZY How many girls did you have sex with before we met?

NICK I forget; I didn't count.

SUZY Yes you did, you said that you'd been to bed with one hundred and six.

ZOE (*Off.*) *Oh my God!*

NICK That was a long time ago I said that. And I was drunk.

SUZY But it was a lot wasn't it? You actually told me how you'd 'done the language schools' when you were at college – remember? You *never* used a condom then! Or am I wrong?

NICK Long time ago

SUZY You actually boasted about it on our first night!

NICK It was a different world then, you know that.

SUZY Women still had babies Nick

NICK Not from me they didn't

SUZY But you don't actually have a clue, do you? Did you ever go back to those one-night stands and check?

NICK Course not, no one did

SUZY Jack had a condom with him.

NICK But he didn't use it!

SUZY But he *will*. Unlike you, he will. You're such a hypocrite. Jack is only a beginner…

NICK Not a beginner at getting trashed so that he's got a hangover that goes on for two days! Not a beginner at being completely mashed when he goes out on a Saturday night!

SUZY We don't know if it's true, it's only what Ben says.

NICK But nor does Jack know! Hours passed that he can't remember because he was so far off his face!

ZOE comes forward.

ZOE He's with a group who are really into using stuff

NICK How long have you been there?

ZOE Since Jack went

NICK (*Rattled.*) Oh. I thought you'd left with him

SUZY She'll cope. Zoe's very mature. Aren't you Zo?

ZOE Yes Mum

SUZY (*To NICK.*) Anyway, you should *talk* to him – not shout and scream – you're close to him and once this blows over, I know he'll listen to you.

NICK Why me? Why not you?

SUZY You're his father Nick. And that's our arrangement.

Pause.

NICK You 'stay out', I 'stay in'?

SUZY Put it how you like, it's too late to change now

NICK Every time I see Jack I want to throw something at him! Help out – I *need* help Suzy. I *can't* talk to him without losing it. I can't manage him.

SUZY Just talk *with* him. You don't have to say anything. Just ask. And listen. See it from his side. I'll talk to him too.

NICK When?

SUZY As soon as I get a chance; I've talked with Zoe a lot. Haven't I Zo?

ZOE Yes Mum.

SUZY We have our 'kitchen conversations'. They're very frank. We talk about everything. (*To ZOE.*) That's right, isn't it?

ZOE Yes Mum

SUZY The first time when you were twelve and quite often since, haven't we?

ZOE Yes

SUZY Have you ever really done that with Jack?

NICK No

SUZY So try it! It's not too late – it will have a big impact. 'Specially coming from you.

ZOE Can I say something?

SUZY Of course

ZOE You do give me a bit of a lecture – is Dad going to do that?

SUZY No of course not. I don't do that do I?

ZOE Yes you do – you go on about *equipment* and all the dangers and risks – I don't think Jack needs that at the moment.

SUZY And just what do you suggest we should do?

ZOE Talk to him about how he's feeling

SUZY Don't patronise me Zoe!

ZOE There you go!

SUZY What do you mean, 'there I go'?

ZOE You get impatient with me when I ask questions. You always do the same thing. You start to move around the kitchen, cutting things in half, onions, bread, meat, you start sawing away, you have to be busy – because you won't talk about feelings, you just carry on, chop, chop, chop. 'You must carry a condom. You must go on the pill.' You never stop, Mum. Your talks are lectures, sex lectures and they're actually the same as the ones we get at school every year. All one-way.

SUZY Right.

ZOE They're not 'conversations'.

SUZY I've got the point.

ZOE Can I say one more thing Mum?

SUZY nods tightly.

He won't trust Dad again for ages

SUZY   No I suppose not

ZOE   So it's important he trusts you

SUZY   Of course Zoe

ZOE   So you have to talk to him.

NICK   Fine by me

ZOE   He's really really upset by how you were to him, Dad.

NICK and SUZY both look at ZOE and say nothing.

I'm going to find him now

SUZY   Yes, thank you Zoe.

Exit ZOE.

I think you are taking out your sexual frustration on Jack.

NICK   Really?

SUZY   Yup. I think fathers aged around forty do it a lot when their boys are becoming young men.

NICK   Who else is there to take it out on when their wives are frigid?

SUZY   There is no way I am frigid.

NICK   Yes you fucking are.

SUZY   Don't 'fucking' me or I'll walk out the door and then you can take out your frustrations in any way you choose.

NICK   I'll talk exactly as I want.

SUZY   You swear too much and you swear at me and at Jack and in front of Zoe. Stop doing it, it's violence and we all know it's that. Of course I freeze up if you come on with all this 'fuck me or I'll shout the fucking house down' stuff. It'd turn off anyone.

NICK   My mouth is a *consequence* of your obsession with your work! I look after you and I look after the family; since they were this small I have been a devoted single fucking mother –

SUZY   There you go again! I mean it Nick – you carry on 'fucking' and I'm going, I'm not staying to be abused by a man who can't talk civilly to his wife – or to his family. Jack is an attractive boy. He is discovering that for himself. If you give

him a break – I mean if you don't smash his confidence
with your tantrums, he'll gain self-esteem. The drugs will
fade out.

NICK   You simply don't know him. You don't know him because
you're never here.

SUZY   You do it your way then.

NICK   I've had no choice. I've always done it my way.

SUZY   Then he'll really give you something to worry about. He'll do
stuff to spite you.
You see how you like that.

NICK   Thanks for your loyal support

SUZY   You are crass, you do know that don't you?

NICK looks at her, shakes his head, stares at the floor.

Can I go now? It may be Sunday but I have some real
problems to sort out at work.

NICK   Oh don't let me hold you up – and please note my good
conduct. I'm not saying 'fuck this!' – or 'fuck off!' – or 'fuck
you!'

SUZY   Prick!

NICK   FUCK YOU VERY MUCH!

Dance / Movement
Music: Adams or Bach

*JACK and ZOE manipulate NICK and SUZY. They place NICK
in the house and SUZY outside it. JACK sits on the house.*

Scene Three

JACK outdoors, alone.

Enter ZOE. ZOE holds out chocolate to him. JACK ignores her.

ZOE   I thought you might be hungry

Silence.

I'm sorry I told Dad

JACK Why did you?

ZOE I'm worried about you and what's happened and what
     Ben said. You've been so miserable, not talking for ages
     and you've done nothing about it. I thought Dad would
     understand.

     Silence.

     I didn't ever think that he'd explode like that.

     ZOE offers chocolate again. JACK declines it.

JACK If Dad talks to me like that again I'm going to hit him Zoe

ZOE Right

JACK If he starts on me like that again, I'm going to punch him

ZOE Mum is furious with Dad.

JACK She should be.

     *He snatches the chocolate and splits it between the two
     of them.*

     You were at the party, right?

ZOE Yeah. For a bit

JACK Did you see me?

ZOE No – there were a lot of people. I never saw you. I left about
     six hours before.

JACK Who with?

ZOE I don't know his name. Honestly

JACK Where'd you go then Zo? You been sleeping around a bit
     yourself?

ZOE No. I went home Jack.

JACK You sure about that?

ZOE YES!

JACK Sure your memory's not playing tricks?

ZOE Just shut up Jack – you're such an idiot

JACK I've told you so much! And you grassed me up.

ZOE I said I'm sorry Jack

     Beat.

JACK So did you?

ZOE What?

JACK You know – the man with no name…?

ZOE No Jack: I didn't – and I wouldn't – and if I meet him again
      – we won't.

JACK Alright!

ZOE Why don't you listen? Why do you never listen to me? Why do
      you only listen to trash like Ben?

JACK I only asked.

ZOE I am not a slag – unlike Beth Green and Sadie Bennett –

JACK Sadie is not a slag

ZOE Just what is she then, Jack? Just what is any girl who has
      sex in a toilet with a boy she hardly knows?

JACK It wasn't in the toilet –

ZOE Whatever!

JACK I do know her

ZOE Not really you don't. And you never will now.

JACK And I really like her

ZOE Which one?

JACK Sadie

ZOE Then why didn't you wait?

JACK Then Ben would have had her! Or Craig maybe.

ZOE She's a slag – and *Ben's* a slag – and *Craig's* a slag – you're
      all slags.

JACK Don't *you* start!

ZOE You're 'King Slag'…

JACK What do you know Zoe?

ZOE I know enough.

JACK No you don't

ZOE Yes I do.

JACK You know shit

ZOE   How can you call Ben a friend?

JACK   How else would I know what happened?

ZOE   Don't you see it's him who makes you do stuff?

JACK   No one makes me do anything

ZOE   He gives you pills and vodka and watches you have sex with
       a girl you don't even know – in a car – and that's you doing
       'your thing', is it Jack?

JACK   It was a crazy night

ZOE   Whatever it was, you've got to talk to Sadie and to Beth

JACK   I *can't*! Even if they were standing in front of me, words
       wouldn't come.

ZOE   Why?

       *JACK shakes his head; if he could tell **ZOE**, he'd tell the
       girls.*

       You don't remember *anything* Jack?

JACK   I remember Sadie and after that it's a complete blank.

ZOE   So what's the point? Why bother having sex if you can't
       remember it? it's supposed to be erotic, Jack.

       JACK stares at the floor.

       'Erotic'…

JACK   What?

ZOE   You ever heard the word 'erotic', Jack?

JACK   Yeah

ZOE   D'you know what it means?

JACK   Yeah

ZOE   What?

JACK   Porn.

ZOE   No it doesn't.
       It means subtle. Subtle pleasure. Sexual pleasure.

JACK   Oh

ZOE   Don't they do that in Sex Ed for boys then?

JACK   We did diseases.

ZOE   That's why everyone gets wrecked. They're afraid of what
      they'll catch. Then they're so wasted, they catch it anyway.

JACK Ta Zo.

ZOE   No one'll ever treat me that way.
      When I first have sex I'm going to remember it.
      And so will he. Whoever he is.

JACK Just because you've never done it doesn't make you special.

ZOE   Yes it does. I am special.

JACK It's all up here with you. In your head. In your diary. You're
      ignorant.

ZOE   I respect myself. I'll stay that way as long as I want. I have a
      choice. Unlike you.

JACK You make me bloody sick

ZOE   You ask for it Jack. It didn't have to happen like this.

      *In frustration, **JACK** starts to jump up and down and to
      run on the spot.*

      Music starts.

      What are you doing?
      Oh my God Jack what are you doing?
      Jack?!

JACK I'm not going home tonight.

ZOE   Where will you stay?

JACK Here.

ZOE   In the woods?

JACK Back to nature.

ZOE   Why Jack? Mum and Dad will be worried. I know they will.
      Don't go Jack!

JACK Fuck them. Fuck you.

ZOE   Jack! Jack! Where are you going? Jack! Come back! Jack
      – I'm sorry! – come back! Jack...

      *At the end **JACK** has 'run away'.*

      ***ZOE** is left alone crying.*

      Segue to:

Dance of the Family: Suzy, Nick, Jack, Zoe
Music: Adams or Bach

ZOE is crying and sits and puts on her shoes.

SUZY wheels her suitcase around the space, leaving home.

JACK curls up into a ball.

NICK pushes the entire house across the stage and then dances a solo.

Finally ZOE goes into the house and NICK sits on the top.

Each member of the family has now fallen out with every other member.

Scene Four

The woods. Night-time.

SUZY enters calling for JACK. She has her suitcase with her.

SUZY Jack! Jack!
Jack, if you are here, please come out. Please!
(*Louder.*) I am getting quite scared in here. SCARED!
Jack! JAAACK!!

JACK (*Suddenly very close / swinging through branches.*) Mum…

SUZY (*Jumps.*) Jack! Is that you?

JACK answers by putting his face right up close to his mother.

What are you doing out here?

JACK Nothing much Mum

SUZY This is not somewhere I want to be Jack – I'm glad I found you – but now let's get out of here!

JACK But it's beautiful Mum – look – the moon, the shadow of the leaves, the breeze – the whole place comes alive now – there's an owl up there, he's really close.

Beat.

SUZY But…

JACK Listen…
Can you hear him?

SUZY   Have you been here before?

JACK   Ben and I used to come up for a smoke – stay here half
       Saturday night – then get into bed before you woke up in
       the morning. Never stayed here the whole night before.

SUZY   You're not doing that?

JACK   Why not? Who comes here at night? Everyone's home
       sleeping sound.

       Beat.

       How did you know I was here?

SUZY   Zoe texted me that you'd run off. That was hours ago. Now
       my tights are ripped and my shoes are soaked. Please can –

JACK   I'm not going home Mum. I'm not. I'm not going home
       because I can't live with him.

SUZY   You're staying the whole night out here?

JACK   Yeah. I'm going back to nature. I am sick of Dad and Zoe and
       you; I am totally sick of you all.

SUZY   So you really are staying here?

JACK   I want to be a wild boy.

SUZY   You've always been wild Jack!

JACK   I'm tame. Tame boy. Everyone please shit on me.

       Beat.

SUZY   Jack?

JACK   Yes?

SUZY   Will you look after me if I stay here with you?

JACK   Of course Mum…
       When were you last in a wood? In the night?

SUZY   I don't remember. A long time ago I think.

JACK   Too long ago; you should try it more often. I only ever see you
       at midnight in the kitchen.

SUZY   I work very hard Jack.

JACK   That's all you ever say. And 'I'm tired'. It's your motto.

SUZY   Well, I am. Tonight won't help either.

JACK   You've been crying.

SUZY   I'm upset

JACK   Because of me?

SUZY   No – because of your Dad.

JACK   You too?

SUZY   Yes

JACK   He's a monster

SUZY   He is.

JACK   You never know when he's going to jump you. Or bite you. Or
        molest you.

SUZY   I know

JACK   I don't know how you put up with him Mum.

SUZY   Nor do I

JACK   See, it's you who's come to find me – not him.
        He doesn't love anyone else.
        He just loves himself.

        SUZY nods.

        He's a fucking tyrant.
        He'll end up living on his own at this rate

SUZY   (*Snaps.*) Jack!

        Silence.

JACK   What's with the bag?

SUZY   Oh just some things for the night – my work stuff –

JACK   (*Fazed.*) Where are you going?

SUZY   I'd just had enough of fighting with your Dad – I packed a
        bag and I walked out of the house

        Beat.

JACK   You've just walked out on Dad?

SUZY   Yes. I thought I may not be much of a wife but I'm still your
        mother. So I came to look for you; but the wood is much
        bigger at night. I got lost.

JACK   You've left Dad?

SUZY Yes

JACK You've *left* him?

SUZY Yes. Just for now.

JACK Then where are you going to live? What'll happen?

SUZY I don't know Jack. It's just happened. I haven't had time to think.

JACK Where will you live?

SUZY I don't know. The Hilton.

JACK Now?

SUZY I suppose it's a bit late to find anywhere now.

JACK But not home?

SUZY I'm not going back!

JACK How can I 'run away' if you follow me, Mum?
I'm meant to be running *from* you – not *with* you!

SUZY I'm sorry Jack – I didn't see it that way

JACK How long before Dad comes running after you?
And Zoe after him?
It's stupid
We'll all end up running away from home.
In a group.

Scene Five

At home.

NICK Jack will be fine Zoe

ZOE How do you know he'll be fine?

NICK It's a warm night

ZOE He might get attacked or mugged

NICK He's a smart boy

ZOE At least we should go and search for him Dad

NICK I really want to be here when Mum gets back

Beat.

ZOE   (*Sceptical.*) What I don't get is why you want to wait to say
         hullo to Mum – who will walk straight past you, make a cup
         of tea and go to bed, probably without saying more than
         about four words – *rather* than go and search for Jack who
         has just run away from home?

NICK   Jack wants to be alone – he'll find his own way back.

         Silence.

ZOE   When is Mum back?

NICK   Not sure – she'll be late

ZOE   And you're staying up?

NICK   Why not?

ZOE   Do you know she's coming back? Did she say?

NICK   We had a bit of an argument

ZOE   You mean she might not come back?

NICK   She'll be back definitely

ZOE   But not tonight?

NICK   Like I say, I'd rather be here.

         Silence.

         Someone called for you when you were out.

         ZOE looks expectant.

         They didn't leave a name

ZOE   Is 'they' a boy?

NICK   Yes.

ZOE   Will he ring back?

NICK   Rang off; didn't say.

         Silence.

         You weren't at that party too were you?

ZOE   Which party?

NICK   The one Jack went to?

ZOE   Yes I was.

NICK Oh.

It's not a complete blank for you as well?

ZOE I've told you I don't do drugs. About a hundred times.

NICK So you didn't come to any harm then?

ZOE 'Come to any harm'; what does that mean?

NICK You know what I mean.

ZOE No I don't, what do you mean?

NICK Well you know what happened to Jack.

Pause.

ZOE No; I didn't come to any harm.

NICK Ask no questions, get no lies?

ZOE Dad, I'm not lying.

NICK Or answering questions?

ZOE What is this, an inquisition, I'm sorry I came to talk to you now.

NICK Alright

He puts his arms out to her; she walks into them, accepts the hug.

That's more like my girl.

ZOE Dad?

NICK Yes angel?

ZOE You don't know where Jack is – or Mum is?

NICK Not at this moment

ZOE It's just you and me?

NICK What do you mean?

ZOE I mean if they both decided to not come back, you and me would be 'the family' – right?

NICK Well it wouldn't happen Zoe so there's not much point speculating

ZOE But if it did?

NICK Well, I'd live here and so would you, so, yes, we would go on being 'the family', yes, I suppose…

ZOE And if I walked out as well, it would be just you?

    NICK does not find a reply.

    I mean, Dad, if we all left you, 'the family' would just be you?

NICK I don't know.
    Perhaps you'd all move back in

ZOE And you'd move out?

NICK Zoe why are you asking this?

ZOE Just trying to keep up Dad

NICK Let's talk about something else shall we?

ZOE I don't mind

NICK Good

ZOE So – did you really shag a hundred and six women?

NICK That's enough. It was a long time ago

ZOE Were you a real stud in your day Dad?

NICK It was a long time ago and I was not a stud.

ZOE So who was your real first, Dad?

NICK (*Sighs.*) It was a girl in the country I walked home when I
    was on a school geography trip. I didn't really know her.
    Apart from that evening. I remember her name was Gale.
    And don't ask me if I had any protection because I didn't.

ZOE What happened?

NICK We lay down by a ditch and it was over in one second and I
    never saw her again.

ZOE Did you walk her home?

NICK I said goodnight

ZOE Did you see her the next day?

NICK No I didn't

ZOE Did you send her flowers instead?

NICK Come on Zoe, I was seventeen

ZOE Don't you cringe when you think about it?

NICK I was over the moon.

ZOE   Don't you cringe now? At yourself? At how mad you get with Jack?

NICK   My Dad would have been the same with me

ZOE   What's that got to do with it?!

NICK   I've had enough of this

ZOE   Was Mum the hundred and seventh?

NICK   Enough!

ZOE   Is she the last one?

NICK moves away, refusing to answer.

ZOE   Is she?

NICK   I said enough!

ZOE   *Is* she enough? Enough for *you*?
       Jack has a lot to learn from you, doesn't he?
       He can learn how *not* to treat women!

NICK   Look Zoe –

ZOE   You're going to give me some advice? Bring me to my senses? Make me hate you as much as Jack does…

ZOE starts hitting him and pummelling him.

       We're not stupid Dad! We know so much more now than you ever did then, you arrogant bloody bastard.

ZOE begins to cry.

She refuses a hug from NICK.

NICK   Look Zoe, listen, listen –
       I love Mum very much.

ZOE   (*Still upset.*) How do you think she feels about you?

NICK   You ask her that Zoe; not me.

ZOE   Alright. I will.

Beat.

NICK   Tell me what she says.

ZOE   Hypocrite! You ask her yourself!

Scene Six

In the woods at night.

SUZY and JACK are lying down and are now very relaxed together. It is clear they have been talking for some time.

JACK I've been mad about Sadie for ages.

SUZY I didn't know.

JACK (*Shrugs.*) But I found her difficult to be with. Not her fault. I always ran out of stuff to say after a minute or so. So I ended up not ever talking to her at all. On the night of the party I had coke for the first time. You should try it Mum. So relaxing. I was so cool when I saw her. I was funny. She's got one of those laughs that you just want to hear more of. And she's a beautiful dancer. Magic.

SUZY You haven't called her?

JACK I want to. But it's over when I phone her.

SUZY Why should it be over?

JACK If I call her I have to tell her everything that happened.

SUZY And then what?

JACK She'll know what I did with Beth and she won't see me again.

SUZY I think you should tell everyone everything.

JACK Mum, you can't do that.

SUZY Tell your family, tell the doctor, tell the girls, tell your friends. Forget all this 'drama', Jack. You're seventeen. You went too far. Say sorry.

JACK And what if Sadie is pregnant Mum?

SUZY Don't wait for her dad to come and find you. Call her.

JACK Were your boyfriends like that? Sensitive?

SUZY Mostly not.

JACK Did you have a lot?

SUZY Yes, of course I did.

JACK Was Dad your first?

SUZY No, definitely not.

JACK So you were experienced when you met him?

SUZY Dad was the first man that I enjoyed – till then it was
       …disappointing

JACK Why Dad?

SUZY He was funny and he was interested in me

JACK Is that all?

SUZY Men so seldom respond to you. They want you to respond
       to them. Your dad gave everything. And he was musical. I
       liked that. I fell in love with him very quickly. Falling in love
       changes everything. It's addictive. Can't get off it.

JACK And you're going to leave him?

SUZY For a night. A night with another man.

JACK Who?

SUZY You, stupid.

       JACK stands up and stretches.

       Where are you going?

JACK I'm disappearing Mum.

SUZY (*Alarmed.*) Where? How long for?

JACK That's the point Mum – I don't know! I came here to be by
       myself for a night. Find out how I feel. Under the stars. All
       alone. Me and a few foxes and birds.
       And then you came along.

SUZY Sorry Jack…

JACK I'm glad you found me Mum. It shows that you care. We
       don't always think you do. Because you're so busy, I mean.

SUZY Of course I care.

JACK And I like seeing you Mum, don't get me wrong.

SUZY Good

JACK This is the longest we've talked, ever.

       JACK leaves SUZY and exits.

       SUZY alone, not sure what to do next.

Scene Seven

*SUZY's mobile rings. She sees it is **NICK** who is calling; she stares at the phone. **SUZY** answers.*

SUZY (*On phone*.) Yes. Hullo.

NICK (*On phone*.) Hullo Suzy. Are you alright?

SUZY Yes. I'm alright. I'm in a lovely place. The sun is rising. It feels good to be alive.

NICK Oh. Where are you?

SUZY In the woods.

NICK Where? On the heath?

SUZY Yes

NICK Just stay where you are, I'll be there in ten minutes –

SUZY Relax. I'm fine. I've spent the night here.

NICK On your own?

SUZY No

NICK Who with then?

SUZY Jack. We talked all night. He looked after me and he made me feel safe.

NICK Oh

Beat.

What are you doing now?

SUZY I'll have a stroll. Take the day off work.

NICK I could come and meet you.

SUZY I want to be alone! It's not Jack and Zoe I'm running from. It's you!

NICK I think you're running from them too.

SUZY Why would I do that? Why would I run from my own children?

NICK I think that you're so needed at work you've decided you're not needed at home.

SUZY is silent.

I don't know when any of you are coming back.

SUZY Zoe's there isn't she?

NICK No.

SUZY Where is she?

NICK She walked out last night. A boy I've never seen before came round in a car and she got in and off she went.

SUZY Where's she gone?

NICK I don't know

SUZY Who is it? What's his name?

NICK I didn't ask

SUZY Why ever not?

NICK Zoe was very angry with me last night; over what I'd said to Jack.

SUZY You don't know who this boy is?! What does he look like?

NICK Tall and dark; well mannered. He knew my name. Then Zoe just walked out and slammed the door without saying goodnight.

SUZY And she hasn't come back?

NICK No.

SUZY She hasn't phoned?

NICK She left her phone here.

SUZY All night? She's fifteen, Nick!

NICK I kept thinking she'd come back.
And then I fell asleep.

SUZY How could you fall asleep?

NICK I don't know.
I didn't even dream.
When I woke up
I realised you'd all left me.

SUZY My God.

NICK I'm sorry for what I've said. How I've been.
Please come back

Movement: Nick, Suzy
Music: Bach

*SUZY returns and she and **NICK** put the house back in place together.*

Following scene continues at same time:

Scene Eight

JACK (*On phone.*) Can I speak to Sadie please?

MAN (*On phone.*) Who is it?

JACK It's Jack

MAN She's doing her homework – can't it wait?

JACK It's quite urgent.

MAN Who are you Jack?

JACK I'm a friend. From Northside.

MAN Sadie! – Phone! It's a boy called Jack…

Sound of Sadie approaching.

SADIE (*On phone.*) Hullo…?

JACK Hullo is that Sadie?

SADIE Yes, it's me, hullo Jack, I'd given up –

JACK Sadie, I'm sorry, I was going to call you but I lost your mobile number –

SADIE It's alright, how you doing?

JACK I'm alright… You?

SADIE Yeah I'm good

JACK You know we were together?

SADIE At Carol Smith's?

JACK Yeah, at the party

SADIE Yeah…

JACK Something I should tell you

SADIE What?

JACK   You know we had sex?

SADIE   Yes Jack, what?

JACK   I've had one or two problems – down below – and…well…
          I've got an STI

SADIE   What's that?

JACK   A sexually transmitted infection

SADIE   Oh

JACK   I checked it out and now I've got some treatment –

SADIE   Is this some kind of horrible joke you're playing?

JACK   No Sadie not at all, I've just come out of the clinic and the
          first thing that they tell you must do is to phone your partner

SADIE   You're not my partner

JACK   I know I'm not but I was then wasn't I? At the time?

SADIE   Why didn't you tell me?

JACK   I'm telling you now aren't I?

SADIE   I thought you had a condom

JACK   I did have a condom

SADIE   Didn't you use it?

JACK   No

SADIE   Why?

JACK   I forgot

SADIE   I don't *believe* this

JACK   I'm really sorry Sadie

SADIE   This is awful

JACK   I can't remember everything properly –

SADIE   Already?

JACK   But I'm right we did, didn't we?

SADIE   Did what?

JACK   Have sex? Together?

SADIE   Yes

JACK   Right. Just want to be sure.

SADIE   What am I supposed to do?

JACK   You should go to the clinic at the hospital. It's no big deal. It's round the back. They just give you a pill. It's simple.

SADIE   I haven't got anything

JACK   It doesn't always show – in women

SADIE   Are you saying you got this disease from me?

JACK   Not exactly – according to Ben I could have got it from you or someone else

SADIE   Who?

JACK   I'm not saying Sadie because I don't know if it's true

SADIE   Ben? Ben Mathews?

JACK   Yeah, Ben…

SADIE   So what did he say?

JACK   Ben says that after we were together, I got totally off my face –

SADIE   What do you mean you could have caught it from someone else?

JACK   According to Ben – after you left the party –

SADIE   I didn't leave – *you* vanished! I looked for you everywhere and I left feeling a slag, just a fuck in the dark and not a word from you since – till this!
'Oh hello Sadie – sorry – you've got AIDS.'

JACK   It's not AIDS! The clinic say it's an infection, you'll be alright if you just go to the clinic

SADIE   Oh shut up about the clinic! What does Ben say happened after I left – who were you with?

JACK   Beth. Beth Green

SADIE   *Beth Green!?* Jack!

JACK   Yup – That's what Ben says. I don't remember a thing about it; I never ever spoke to Beth Green. Ben says that I also –

SADIE   I don't want to know Jack!

JACK   You asked me!

SADIE   Don't call me again!

JACK   Well now you know. I'm really sorry Sadie, I didn't want to upset you but now you know.

SADIE   And why do you think *I* gave it to *you*? – it sounds more like *you* gave it to *me* – and half the other girls who were at the party!

JACK   Aren't you exaggerating?

SADIE   You don't know what you're doing, do you Jack? You're not even responsible for your own actions – you don't even know where you put it, you idiot!

JACK   Look Sadie –

SADIE   I hope you caught it from Beth Green!

JACK   Listen…

SADIE   I hope you die!

JACK   Sadie!

SADIE   Oh fuck off Jack!

Music: Bach

ZOE returns home and goes straight to her room. Her parents come to her room together.

Scene Nine

NICK   Zoe, just where the hell have you been?

SUZY   We've been worried sick!

NICK   We haven't a clue where you've been or what you've done.

ZOE   Where's Jack? Is he back?

SUZY   I talked to Jack last night. He is coming home.

ZOE   When?

SUZY   I don't know when exactly but I absolutely trust him to come home

ZOE   Where is he now?

SUZY   I don't know Zoe; he's seventeen, I can't stalk him you know.

ZOE   Why do you stalk me?

SUZY   We don't stalk you, you're younger and you're a girl and we love you

NICK   We just want you to be safe

NICK goes over and puts his arm around ZOE.

I'd never have got over it if something'd happened to you. I'm so relieved you're alright

ZOE   Are you, Dad?

NICK   So are we going to meet him?

ZOE   Maybe

NICK   Then what's his name?

ZOE   That's my business

NICK   He looked after you, anyway?

ZOE   Yeah, he 'looked after me'.

NICK   I hope he did

ZOE   You hope he did? Perhaps *I* did.
Perhaps I looked after myself…
You are so condescending

NICK   I am not condescending.

ZOE   Oh you are, Dad, you are!

NICK starts to fume.

NICK   Don't speak to me like that!

ZOE   Both of you now trust Jack but you don't trust me.
That shows how little you know about either of us.

Beat.

SUZY   (*Peacemaker.*) We will talk properly Zoe, you and I
Talking to Jack all night has made a difference Zoe.

ZOE   What did you talk about? You and Jack?

SUZY   About us all. About Dad

Beat.

ZOE   And how do *you* feel about Dad?

SUZY   What kind of question is that?

ZOE   Dad asked me to ask you

SUZY   (*Looks to **NICK**.*) Did he?

          NICK nods, eyes to ceiling.

ZOE   Yes, Mum, he did.

SUZY   Dad and I are discussing things at the moment. Positively.

ZOE   He told me what he feels about you

SUZY   I don't know if I want to know what he said to you

ZOE   He said he loves you very much.
          He asked me to ask you how you feel about him.

SUZY   When I know how I feel, you'll be the first person to know

ZOE   Don't tell me Mum. Tell Dad. It's him who needs to know.

SUZY   (*Explodes.*) DON'T TELL ME WHO I AM AND WHAT I AM AND
          WHAT I'M MEANT TO FEEL! IT DRIVES ME INSANE!

          ZOE goes to exit and SUZY stops her.

          I know you mean well, but I'm not perfect, Zoe. People like
          me get it wrong. I want you to accept that. It's strange but
          sometimes the simplest things are the hardest – like telling
          the person you love most that you love him. I know I'm not
          good at talking about emotions but it doesn't mean I don't
          have any. Quite the opposite sometimes. D'you see?

          ZOE is upset. She nods and embraces SUZY.

Music: Bach

          NICK, SUZY and ZOE scatter through the house.

          Following scene goes on simultaneously:

Scene Ten

JACK   (*On phone.*) Hullo is that Beth Green? Hi, this is Jack – Ben's
          mate? Yeah – Hi – you probably know why I'm ringing you

– it's about that party a few weeks ago – I really don't know exactly how to say this and I want to say sorry in advance of what I've got to say – because I know it sounds really bad and – anyway to cut to the chase, as they say, I *know* what happened and I'm sorry, I'm *really* sorry but because of it I have been to the clinic, the clinic behind the hospital – it's quite difficult to find – and I've had a test and I've got a *very* mild infection that needs just antibiotics. They give them to you on the spot. So you must go there and I *have* to tell you that – they said I had to. Okay? Sorry.

BETH (*On phone*.) I wasn't at that party.

JACK Oh

BETH I couldn't go because it was my auntie's birthday party.

JACK But…

BETH Her sixtieth birthday party.

JACK Right…

BETH I don't know what you're talking about.

JACK But – but –

BETH Fuck off Jack – I wouldn't have sex with you however pissed I was

   Beth hangs up on him. **JACK** *explodes in rage.*

Dance: Jack
Music: 'Certain Romance' by Arctic Monkeys

   JACK *collapses in a heap on the floor with his iPod.*

Scene Eleven

   NICK *enters.*

JACK What are you staring at me for?

NICK I'm glad I found you – are you alright?

JACK NO I AM NOT ALRIGHT. NOT AT ALL.

NICK I'm sorry Jack, I feel I'm to blame –

JACK YES! YOU ARE!

NICK What happened?

JACK The doctor said I had to phone my partner, so I called Sadie
      and I told her

NICK That's good, Jack

JACK I told her what I'd got and I told her about Beth as well

NICK That's good too. What'd she say?

JACK She told me to fuck off

NICK Right

JACK Then I called Beth

NICK What'd she say?

JACK She said fuck off too, only stronger than Sadie. She was
      never at the party. Ben made the whole thing up.

NICK I'm not surprised

JACK You believed Ben!

NICK Maybe I did.

JACK You did! But one of the reasons I couldn't remember having
      sex with her is because I didn't have sex with her!

NICK So Ben made it all up?

      JACK nods.

      I'd like to get my hands on him.

JACK So where was your support yesterday Dad!?

      Pause.

NICK He's your best friend, isn't he?

JACK He was.

NICK I'm sorry Jack

JACK I can't believe he's done this to me.

NICK Why did he?

JACK I don't know. You *both* want to do me in. What's wrong? With
      me?

NICK Perhaps he's jealous of you

JACK Ben? I don't think so

NICK Why not? You're good-looking; you're funny; you're popular.
I'm sure girls find you attractive

JACK Are you serious?

NICK Of course I am
You're going to be a threat to guys like Ben.

JACK Ben can have who he wants

NICK I wouldn't be so sure.
Can he have Sadie?

JACK He doesn't fancy her.

NICK Oh doesn't he?
A lot of guys are like that.
Very cocksure on the surface but when it comes down to it
They're jerks
They're competitive and spiteful,
They'll do anything to put one over on you.

*JACK surveys **NICK**.*

JACK Maybe he does fancy Sadie

NICK He is totally in awe of you Jack
He fears you
You should feel good about yourself
You're a great lad

JACK Why didn't you talk with me like this yesterday Dad?
Why did you have to behave like a mad dog?

NICK I don't know

JACK I'm not like you Dad.

NICK I know. I know that now. You're completely different.

**Dance: Nick, Jack, Suzy, Zoe
Music: Adams**

Scene Twelve

SIXTH SUNDAY

ZOE (*To audience.*) It's Sunday.
I'm writing my diary for the week while it's calm
Mum and Dad aren't up yet
I fed the cat
Jack is asleep…

It seems the more sex that people have
The less they know what to do about it.
Perhaps the less you know the more you see.

I like my boyfriend
He respects me.
The way I am.
So far…
He makes me feel so good.
I wear his scent now.
Smell…

Mum and Dad think I stayed out all night with him
But I didn't
He drove me to Sophie's house
And I stayed there
We chatted all night and watched *Grease*.

Scene Thirteen

JACK I'm trying to behave as normally as I can.
It's Sunday and I'm at home.
I went to the park with some mates yesterday,
Just to play a game of football.
Our side lost.
Saw Ben there.
He said hi.
I just kind of nodded back.
Zoe said I should have punched him.

He shrugs.

Got a letter yesterday.
It was delivered by hand.
'Dear Jack,
I know I was upset when you called.
Who wouldn't be?
But after what you said, I went to the clinic.
I did have an infection. I was so surprised.
I've only ever been with one other boy.
He's a good friend of yours and you can probably guess who
    he is.
I really want to say thank you.
You said before that that you didn't have my mobile number
So I've put it at the bottom of this letter.
With much love
Sadie (Bennett)'

Scene Fourteen

SUZY   I understand that you might have had enough.
       Of me, I mean. Always needing more sleep.

NICK   Not really

SUZY   You might want to have an affair?

       NICK is silent.

       I mean you probably are having an affair and you're not going
           to tell me

NICK   I haven't got the time.

SUZY   Is that it? You just haven't the time?

NICK   I did try to start up an affair, Suzy.
       Once.

SUZY   Did you?

NICK   Yes. What's the point in lying? I did.
       It never got started though.

SUZY   Oh?

NICK   And it never will

SUZY   Why?

NICK   You're always in the way.
       You're always there…

SUZY   Oh

    Beat.

NICK   Have you had an affair?

SUZY   I wouldn't do that, Nick.
       If I wanted someone else, I'd leave you.
       It's as simple as that.
       And I don't want someone else.
       I want you.

Dance of the Family: Suzy, Nick, Jack, Zoe
Music: Adams or Bach

    The End.

RISK

for Teresa Ariosto

Background

Risk is about 'letting the body talk'. It is a subject particularly suited to dance and to movement. Many young people are looking for ways to feel more alive. How else can they discover their limits? How else can they find out who they are? There is such an abundance of narrative material, which springs from this area of thrill seeking and danger, it was important to find a clear analytical framework to contain the various stories and experiences that we selected from interviews and conversations in Glasgow.

I have concentrated on the choices that many of the teenagers I met in Glasgow have to make when they are still very young. One boy is a successful young criminal at fifteen – but at fifteen he yearns for the freedom his (relatively) innocent mates enjoy. A young girl drinks very heavily at sixteen but questions whether she is doing this for her own pleasure or simply to be accepted by her friends. Another girl is bullied and becomes an even greater bully herself. These young people all take big risks and face big choices.

Each of the characters that we meet in *Risk* go to the brink and know what is involved if they wish to become the agent of their own destiny. Many people do not experience this in a whole lifetime. That is why the choices that Paul, Annmarie, Ed, Michelle and Martin make are not only of significance to themselves but to us as well.

As school begins to dominate children's lives, adult society aims to reduce as much as possible the personal risks that children and their teachers might take. Health and Safety rules are dutifully applied. Schools, homes and playgrounds try very hard to be safe environments. Is there a connection between this 'risk-prevention' and the degree to which young people are drawn to danger, perhaps more than ever before?

Sean Morrissey, a sociologist at the University of Aberdeen (and a former break-dancer) who was present at many of our rehearsals for *Risk*, wrote the following in his daily notes after one of our early workshops:

> The cost of risk, the issue of resources is interesting. In order to take socially acceptable risks, you need to have money, you need to have transport, you need to have internet access in order to book your extreme skiing holiday in Canada, you need to know what you are doing and feel at home amongst the other people you are 'escaping' with. If you do not have these capital resources you have to resist in other ways. You steal a car or climb a pylon. The differences between the former and the latter include the following: a) socially acceptable vis-à-vis deviant; b) bravery vis-à-vis thuggery; c) organised vis-à-vis chaotic;

d) safety harness vis-à-vis no safety harness; e) legal vis-à-vis illegal; f) likely to result in kudos vis-à-vis likely to result in arrest.

I would like also to acknowledge 'The Anthropology of Adolescent Risk-taking Behaviours' (in *Body and Society* (2004)) by the eminent French anthropologist David Le Breton.

Characters

PAUL, the Gambler

ANNMARIE, the Opponent

MARTIN, the Prisoner

MICHELLE, the Fighter

ED, the Rebel

and

FIVE INNOCENTS *played by the same actors*

DESIGN: A dance floor. Audience on three sides.

CHARACTER NOTES:

The Gambler's objective is to survive: is at risk, so takes bigger risks to come out on top.

The Opponent's objective is to be herself: chooses between physical risk and identity risk.

The Prisoner's objective is to leave his front door: has extreme perception of risk.

The Fighter's objective is to have control: overcomes fear of risk.

The Rebel's objective is to find himself: gains self-knowledge through risk.

Risk was first performed at the Tron Theatre, Glasgow, on 8 February 2007 with the following company:

Paul Corrigan
Martin Docherty
Michelle Edwards
Annmarie Fulton
Edward McGurn

Director / Text John Retallack
Director / Choreography Andy Howitt
Musical Arrangement Dave Boyd
Lighting Kai Fischer
Costume Co-ordination Annmarie Fulton

The text was commissioned by macrobert, Scotland's leading arts centre for young people, in association with Company of Angels, Y Dance and the Tron Theatre. The project was supported by the Scottish Arts Council and The Gannochy Trust.

Risk

Instructions to Baby-sitters in Peacetime

CHORUS Keep doors and windows locked at all times. Never open the door to strangers. Do not boil water. Lock up all medicine, bleaches, household cleaners. Running on stairs can lead to fatalities. Accordion-style gates with diamond-shaped openings can entrap a child's head, causing strangulation. Bathing a baby calls for utmost care; aside from the risk of hot water scalds, there is the danger of drowning. Small pieces of food, coins, pins and tiny toys with small removable parts can lodge in the baby's throat and cause choking. The seams of poorly constructed stuffed dolls or animals can break open and release small pellets that can be swallowed or inhaled, causing asphyxiation. Pins and staples on dolls' clothes, hair and accessories can easily puncture or tear a child's skin. Toy caps can produce sounds at noise levels that can damage hearing. Baby-walkers can scoot down a flight of stairs, onto a hot stove or a chip pan or into a glass door. Cribs with decorative knobs on the cornerposts can be a strangulation hazard.

Five Innocents

BOY AGED 13 Last year I organised to do a stunt with my pals, and he was going to videotape it for the internet. At the start it was just a laugh and I wasn't really going to go through with it but then it got serious and…you just want to go through, so I volunteered for it. On the day it took quite a while before I actually went through. The stunt was to jump, I had to jump out the window from the tenth floor of a flat onto all these boxes of cardboard and stuff. I thought I was going to be fine and all that, but when I got up to it I thought I was going to die when I leaped. So when I got down it was a relief. But I broke my arm.

GIRL AGED 12 In May, at my wee sister's communion, em…like…all the rest of my family were all drunk. So I decided to take a bottle of, em…White and McKay's from the cupboard and,

em…when I was goin' to get it, I felt pure nervous like…
'cause I'd never really stolen anything before. And I was
feart in case, like, my mum caught me 'cause then she'd
pure shoot me or something. So like, I was nervous when
I was gettin' it. And then I got it. And my mum never…no
one seen me. So I took it out, and, was dead proud of
myself after that for doin' it. And then, like, I drank it all.
And then, I don't really remember anythin' much after that.

BOY AGED 12   Me 'n' ma pals took a trolley from Tesco's and ah got in it
and ah got my combats stuck in the mesh and they pushed
me full speed down that steep hill by sauchiehall street 'n'
ah crashed inta ah wall and when I fell oot ah gashed ma
leg wide open – I wanted a rush, and I tell ya I got it – it
was FUN man, it was good with no precautions, I got a rush
even though it hurt so much.

GIRL AGED 11   I came home really late on my own and I'd lost my phone
so I couldn't tell my mum where I was. That was my worst
risky moment, being alone on the street at night. My mum
belted me.

BOY AGED 11   Me and my friend were down at the old shut down school
and we were smashing windows and were smashing them
and smashing them for about ten minutes. Then when we
looked behind us was the police. They gave us a bollocking
and were going to take us down to see our mums and dads.
And well that's when I started crying. I cried and cried so
much they let me off with it. It was brilliant.

DANCE / MUSIC.

Voices (1)

Spoken during dance:

CHORUS   My parents never ask anything
They don't care what I do
As long as I stay in
My mum just wants me to pass everything.
I've got two phones, one for Mum, one for Dad.
I'm treated like a baby.
They won't let me do anything.

I've sat in the back
Of my mum's car or my dad's car
Since I was born.
They don't want me to travel
Any other way…

Paul's Story (1)

Solo with movement.

PAUL I hate losing
I love winning

If I take a risk
I'm gonna take the biggest risk
Because if you're gonna get caught
You're as well getting caught for something major

D'y'know what I mean?

'What'd you get caught for?'
'Oh it was just a wee thing'
I think if you're gonna get caught
You've gotta get caught for something that's worth getting
   caught for

Embarrassing to be caught for a wee thing.
You go down this road
You get caught for stealing a mars bar –
That's quite embarrassing

I'm not into scaring up some old lady
I want to go into something better than that
Something you go into smartly dressed
Somewhere you look the part an' all
A con artist
A manipulator
Up with the big boys really
Up with Mr Scorsese and his crew

I'm a learner
I'll take things on
But one thing I know –
The part of being caught
Isna' part of learning

Those who get caught
Are not very good at what they're doing.

In order to succeed
Don't get caught.
If you get caught at something,
You've not thought it through enough.
You might want it
But you don't respect it.

If you don't get caught
You're doing something right.
Some birds are not meant to be caged
Their feathers are just too bright

It's so easy to make a bit o' extra money
A little deal here, a little deal there
You don't need a bank to break into
Or a train to hold up
Just be on hand for your friends
For their everyday needs.

If they want it
You provide it.
If they can't find it
You supply it.
If a stranger asks
Just deny it
It's so easy
If you plan ahead.

Analyse the situation
Weigh the odds
Don't rush
Keep breathing
Hold the eye
Smile, pocket, turn, and walk
Know when to disappear
Don't draw attention to yourself
Discreet you hear
DISCREET
You think I'm having this conversation with you
But I'm not

I'm doing something else
Something else entirely.
It's so easy,
It's so cool

If it's raining
You wear a raincoat.
If you've got a thirst
Then quench it –
Don't eat a biscuit,
That won't fix it

You see a high-energy situation
You step back
Simplicity
Go with the flow

It's both what you do
And how you do it.

I know I'm cocky
Why shouldn't I be?
I've got something to be cocky about.

Know Jack and the Beanstalk?
The boy who steals the gold from under the giant's nose?
He took one BIG RISK
I took a risk like Jack
I stole not one gold piece but a few from under the nose
Of a wee big man.
A wee big man with the power of a giant
A man who could snap me like that
Snap my back
Like the giant
Snapped Jack

I got my gold and I got away

What next?
Did I buy a car?
Too young
Did I buy a trip?
Got school
Some bling?
Too loud

Some clothes?
That's nice, where did you find the money for *that*?
It's no good
You draw attention to yourself –
And then you get caught.

I get everything I want and
I do nothing with it.
Having a lot of money is a bigger risk
Than having none.

Like I say
The part of being caught
Isna' part of learning
Those who get caught
are not very good at what they're doing.

One day there is a knock on the door.
I open it.
I wish I never had.

Jack has to give the gold back
But before he gives the gold back
Jack gets a smack.

I'd sooner do ten years inside
Than what they'd do to me the next time.
I live with the watchfulness of a man with four kids
And a debt-collector at his door.

I'm fifteen.
I want to sleep at night
And go to school in the morning.

D'y'know what I mean?

DANCE / MUSIC.

Voices (2)

CHORUS   I am what I breathe
I am what I eat
I depend on others
I do not know what tomorrow will bring

Annmarie's Story (1)

*Solo with dancing. **ANNMARIE** is a 'social' dancer. She knows her steps better than anyone else.*

ANNMARIE It was the first time I went out in a group with my friends.
It was a really big club, 'The Garage'.
Everyone was taking something,
All my friends were out off their faces
I was sober and I didn't snog anyone.
I just danced all night.
Every time we all went out together,
It seemed to go like that.
They all got wiped out and I didn't.
I never drank or took anything.
Some of my friends started on at me –
Why was I cool and in control, always?
While they were getting wrecked?
Was I mean? Or scared?
Why was I always such a good girl?
I said to them I like clubbing,
I'm having a great time –
Leave me alone.
And it was always me who was there
To scrape the puke from out their hair,
To protect them from blokes,
To tell them where they lived
And I got them home too, by cab;
They wouldn't remember that the next day
Or believe that it had cost a tenner.
They thought I just wanted to be in control of them;
I was too scared to 'let go'.
I said I let go completely when I'm dancing.
They said I never joined in.
That was rubbish and I told them so
And I just kept on dancing.
But they didn't leave off.
They started to wind me up.
They said I was a goody two-shoes.
They called me a stuck-up.
Well that was too much.
I am not stuck-up.

So one night I had a pint and a smoke –
In front of them all.
They all gasped and cheered.
I went to the toilet and threw up.
When I came back they were all watching to see what I'd do.
I bought a round and had another pint.
My rating went right up.
They hugged me, congratulated me.
After that whenever I went out with them,
If they got pissed, I got pissed with them.
And I couldn't remember how I got home,
Or what I'd said or what I'd done or who I'd done it with.
Thing was, it seemed a bigger risk to be sober than be drunk.

And once I'd started drinking, I stopped dancing.

Playground Risk for Children in Peacetime (1)

CHORUS   In playgrounds, children do the unexpected. Little people
do not see risk. Never climb up the front of a slide. Hanging
rings are dangerous to small children. Their heads may be
small enough to go through the ring, turning it into a hanging
noose. Make sure surfaces around playground equipment
have at least twelve inches of wood chips or mulch
underneath them; check the matting is made of safety-tested
rubber.

DANCE / MUSIC.

Voices (3)

1 Don't tell me what to do
   I'll do what I like
   It's my life

2 Sprayed the whole carriage man
   No one does it like us, we are the best

3 Stole a Mercedes and dumped it
   I did a hundred miles an hour

4 Got them on the way home – just two of them – whacked
    'em hard
   There's blood on my shoe and it's not mine

5 I saw the train-driver's eyes – *that* close
   It was amazing, totally mental

6 I won my bet
   I ran across six lanes – scary

DANCE / MUSIC.

Martin's Story (1)

*The following is performed on an open stage without any props
at all.*

*MARTIN is an 'anorak' mid-way between comic (Charlie Chaplin)
and tragic (Woyzeck). He lives many floors up.*

MARTIN is lying asleep in bed.
He wakes up.

MARTIN Today's the day!
        I can feel it
        Today's the day!

        He ticks off the day on a chalkboard.

        Thirty-three days
        What's it like outside?

        He opens the curtains.

        Baltic!
        Trees bending in the wind

        He washes his hands.

        I must check my emails.
        Perhaps I'll get that special one I'm waiting for.

        He clicks on computer.

        Three new messages
        Hotmail staff, blah dee blah
        Sainsbury's online, thank you for shopping with us, blah blah
        Final one
        Marie!
        'Dear you, dada dada da, it would be great for us to meet
          tonight at 7 PM at the Glasgow Film Theatre…'

        He jumps away from computer in shock.

She wants to meet after only three months!
That's pretty soon
Wonder what she's like
She's nice, I know she is through speaking to her
Well not speaking to her
Through email, you know, same thing
'Marie' – sounds foreign, French maybe, probably black hair,
  dark eyes
Hmm…nice.

But what if she's big?
You know, large?
And what if she's tall, that would look stupid,
Wee me, big her.
Will she like me?

Does she fancy guys who do this?

He scratches his arm.

Or this?

He scratches his leg.

What will I wear?
Jeans? My polo neck?
Might get too itchy
Could wear my new boots
Well, they're not new, about a year old, but I haven't worn
  them
Will she like a guy in boots?

Maybe she likes big men
Tall men, muscle men, beefcakes…
What if she likes dark men?
I'm not even white
I'm pale blue…

Stop fretting
I could go on a trial run
See how long the bus takes
Check if there are any weirdos about

Just need to put my jacket on
Go to the door
Open the locks

Go outside

He goes to the door.

I've got seven locks
But don't think I'm a prisoner
They're on the inside not the outside
I can open them and go out

He pulls open each lock.

One, two, three, four's a bit stiff, five, six and seven is the
    hardest

He opens the door and stands there, looking out, afraid to move.

All you need to do is to go outside
What's the matter?
Unsure of where to go?

*He crosses to the window, anxious to put distance between
himself and the open door.*

I can come here to the window and see my path
Down the stairs, out the close, turn right, past the people at
    the bus stop and carry on going into the centre of the city
And then the people will laugh at me, stare at me, point at
    me for wearing this disgusting horrible jacket which went
    out of date in the last century!

He tears off the jacket, hurls it to the floor and stamps on it.

This is going to be a great relationship
Marie and I
I'll bring her here to meet my friends

He mimes her coming into his flat through the open door.
He escorts her round the flat.

In you come Marie
I'd like you to meet my friends
This is Mr Sink
Who I see every morning
This is Mr Fridge
Who's alright but a bit frosty
And this is Mr Mirror who's usually very grumpy
But in a very good humour today

He gets to the computer.

And here is my best friend
My special friend,
My oldest, closest friend
My computer

I was going to give him a name
But I thought that'd be a wee bit naff

Oh did I tell you about my seven allergies?
To go with my seven locks?

Asthma – breathing
Eczema – scratching
Washing powder – sneezing
Bananas – puking
Acrylic – rash attack
Salt – palpitations
Nuts – kill me

He starts feverishly to re-bolt the door.

Do you find me attractive Marie?
I bet you can't wait to meet a man
Who can't keep his door open for more than forty-five
   seconds
Who's got seven locks on it to keep people out
The fourth one which is a bit stiff and
The seventh one which is the most difficult to shut

I bet you can't wait to start a long loving relationship
With a guy who hasn't left his house for thirty-three days!

He jumps back into his bed and closes his eyes.

DANCE / MUSIC.

Voices (4)

CHORUS   My body is mine and belongs to no one else
I am responsible for my body
I avoid unncesessary risk
My body is civilised

Michelle's Story (1)

MICHELLE When I was thirteen, my family moved house.
I went from a school with only twenty-five in a class,
One class in each year to a large school in Glasgow –
Oh my God what a shock.
I was the perfect choice for a big bully campaign
By the not so posh and even if I do say so myself –
Not so beautiful girls.
They say jealousy is what makes them bully.
Well after about six months to a year of torment –
Hair being singed on the bus,
Pushed against the wall in the corridor and
Living in utter fear of everyone,
I'd had enough –
I took a RISK.
'Square go right now.'

Lorraine, the hardest girl in my year was the ring leader –
Built like a boy and she even had a skinhead.
She'd been asking for a fight for a month now –
From somewhere deep inside I said it –
'Okay after school'.
There was a large gathering
My heart was beating from my neck,
With no colour and lots of colour flashing back and forward
  on my face.
Well, I marched up,
It was this or a lifetime –
Five more years of her!
Right!

I said I have had enough of this pish from you and
I want it to stop –
She went for me and I for her,
Only I had long locks of hair to pull and she had none.
But I was so riled up
Somehow like superwoman I found strength and –
More than that –
Reason to tunnel my feeling into power.
I went for it, grabbing her, hitting her and kicking her.

Onto the road we went and she even hurled me in front of a
    car.
People cheering young thirteen year-old girls
Like men at a blood sport a hundred years ago.

Well I came out of it alright, a little less hair and a few
    bruises.
And with a lot of respect I hadn't been beaten to a pulp –
I didn't die.
I was an equal match to her –
Or so it seemed.
She ended by telling me I was cool and wasn't a snob
As I had a square go.
If my friends in Perth had seen me
They wouldn't have believed it was me.
I never hit anyone in my life before that.
Now I'd done it, I'd faced up to my fear and my fear had
    gone.
I'd tasted blood and suddenly I wanted more action in my
    life.
Lorraine and her friends said I could join them and they'd
    protect me.
On one condition;
I dropped my friends.
Did I have a choice?
Not really.
So that's what I did.

I became Lorraine's friend.
In some ways, I became Lorraine.
I started to torment and bully people like me.
Well, like I *was*.
I cut my hair really short and I changed my look.
I bought boots with steel caps.
I gave lip to everyone, always kept that little element of
    surprise.
People didn't know what I'd do next.
Up till then I was so clean.
I had a clean past and a clean record.
These girls had marks all over their bodies for all kinds of
    reasons.

I had a lot of catching up to do;
I was accepted and I wanted it to stay that way.
I'd had enough of being kicked around like a pig's bladder.

I managed to keep up my studies
But with constant talks from teachers who were worried
  about me –
'You're on a slippery slope, young lady.'
You'd think my parents'd have noticed or said something
But they were way too busy.
Long hours, big salaries.

I had access to all kinds of sports, skiing holidays,
Surfing with cousins who had a house by the beach,
I had an elder brother who was into climbing and canoeing –
Not for me.
My extreme sport was Lorraine and her mates;
Drugs, drink, skiving, smoking –
Jumping on dirt bikes with boys
Speeding down a canal path at fifty miles per hour.
Charging at twenty kids from the local Catholic school with
  chibs –
Violence and having no choice but to take risks –
Doing what I had to do to be accepted.
And loving every minute.

DANCE / MUSIC.

Voices (5)

*Dance for company with no speaking. Recorded adult voices of
different nationalities: French, English, Scottish, German.*

FRENCH MALE It's over. I've got to the North Pole by skiing on a dream. It's
calling me on, tears of exhaustion are burning my eyes. It's
an unbelievable night, the extreme of marvellous, divine.

FRENCH FEMALE I feel free. I understood what I had to do. The desert is
another zone. It is not we human beings who set the rules.
I thank the Sahara for helping me to achieve my desire.

YOUNG ENGLISH MALE Through all the lights,
Over the pedestrian precinct,
Against the one-way,

> Into the shopping mall,
> See their faces, unbelievable,
> Down the steps,
> Crashed into war memorial,
> Got sent down for nine months.

ENGLISH MALE The hunger, the cold, the tiredness, so what? The moments of total happiness were so powerful. Sometimes it's so beautiful you cry in the moonlight, surfing the waves. There is nothing more to say. The Atlantic is there. Had to sail it. That's all.

SCOTTISH MALE I am a guerrilla in a war I have invented. The enemy is me, my physical weaknesses – and the temptation to give up. That is why I run the triathlon.

I can experience the emotions that society denies me.

YOUNG ENGLISH FEMALE

> I smashed the plate-glass window of McDonald's with a fire axe
> Police charge,
> Kicked one so hard I hurt my foot,
> Jumped from first floor onto bus roof,
> Everyone cheering,
> And –
> 'Body first' –
> I jumped and surfed the crowd.
> I got the shakes about four hours later.

SCOTTISH MALE Sky-diving only feels right when I have goose pimples. It's a gut need. It's a sort of drug. In fact I have to frighten myself.

GERMAN MALE You can only be free when you have nothing to lose

> I'm the dude that surfed the bullet train
> Across Germany at three hundred kilometres per hour
> Stuck to the back with an industrial suction cup
> I filmed myself
> Over a million hits
> The world knows 'Trainrider'
> I rest in peace

DANCE / MUSIC.

Ed's Story (1)

ED My mum and dad live in a flat in Dennistoun in Glasgow.
Me and my brothers,
Andrew, four years older, and Fraser, he's two years older,
Shared a room most of the time I lived at home.
Fraser was a slob and left everything everywhere.
I'm the opposite.
I like everything in its place.
'Specially my books.
Fraser couldn't stand me.
He hated that people knew I was his brother.
I avoided Fraser at school.
Andrew was alright, but on his own.
He was a tearaway and got into a lot of trouble.
He vandalized property, had fights, got drunk, stole stuff,
   crashed cars.
He got away with it, just.
I heard my dad say,
'Boys will be boys; he'll grow out of it.'

Andrew grew out of it.
He's got a job in Aberdeen now and his wife's expecting.
Fraser's engaged, poor girl is all I can say.
They'll all be going home for Christmas.
Loved and respected by their adoring mum and dad.

My dad didn't think I was fit.
Fit for survival.
It bothered him that I didn't get into fights.
He once said, half-joking,
'Why can't you come home with a black eye and a bleeding
   lip like your brothers? Vandalize something, show you're a
   man.'
Instead, I came home with an earring.
You'd think I'd come home in women's clothing.
The whole family went mental.
I took it out before one of them tore it out.
My mother told me off for upsetting my dad.

I was upset but I was pleased too.
It was the first time I felt I had any power at home.

The next day Fraser beat me up.

Neither Andrew or my dad stopped him.

Mum pretended not to hear.

Fraser took the earring and threw it down the sink.

Then everything carried on like it normally did.

We had supper and no one talked about what had just
  happened.

If I said anything they said,

'Oh stop moaning Ed',

'Put it behind you',

'Think yourself lucky, wee man' and

'Next time you'll feel it'.

Then they watched the match and ignored me.

From that day, I stopped talking at home.

And eating.

I just sat there at meals and stared ahead.

I ignored them.

One day, after school, I stayed out till ten.

When I came home, no one asked me where I'd been.

They were all in bed but I didn't speak to anyone at breakfast
  either.

But it wasn't just me ignoring them.

They were ignoring me.

It was a pact.

A silent one.

For over a year, the long silence held between me and my
  family.

Andrew went off to Aberdeen.

I was free to come and go as I pleased and to eat,

But I hardly ate anything at home.

I lost weight.

I used to look at my skinny wrists and I felt great

When I looked at their big necks and their fleshy arms.

After a bit I couldn't eat at home and I didn't want to be there
  either.

I was a stranger at home.

I stayed out till late every night.

I knew how to be alone.

That was my strength, my gift.

I was getting to know the city so well because I was walking
  all over it.
Every night.
I'd walk down Kelvin Walkway, cut through Blythswood
  square through the centre down to Saltmarket,
And then to Glasgow Green.
Here was a shortcut through the Necropolis. Through the city
  of the dead and back to the dead people.

When it rained I'd go into a church and sit in there for a bit.
Sometimes I'd fall asleep.
There's no rule to say kids can't do these things.
I'd come home by eleven, maybe twelve.

The whole city was mine.
I could do what I liked,
I knew the way everywhere.
I knew every bus and every route by heart.
If it was very wet,
I just sat on a bus and watched the streets pass by.
If it was fine I walked where I wanted.
If I got nervous I ran fast for five minutes and
Put a mile between me and a shadow.

Some teenagers are invisible.
I was one.
I was the ghost of Glasgow.

I learnt from my school that my mum and dad thought I was
  a drug addict.
Fraser spoke.
He said I was a pervert.
I broke my silence.
I told them I was a virgin.
That I had never drunk alcohol or taken drugs.
They stared at me.
I said that I was a stranger in my home
I said the only place I felt at home was the street.
This home was completely sterile and they were all dead
  people.
That I'd rather be homeless.
My mother started crying and couldn't stop.
My dad really lost it then.

He started calling me a whole lot of names.
He lashed out at me and I fell over.
My mother started crying and Fraser pulled Dad off me;
That was the only kind thing he's ever done.

MUSIC / DANCE.

Voices (6)

1 CHORUS   I'm bored
This place is dead
It's full of dead people
I don't want to be like them

2 CHORUS   I'm well respected by my peers at school
My mates think the world of me
My mum and dad are happy together
They love and respect me
They give me the freedom and trust
I deserve…
I pass your exams
I see yourself ten years from now.
I'm the future.
I'm got a plan
I'm sound
I'm not in danger
I know where I'm going.

Risk is for those less fortunate than me.
Risk is for others.

3 CHORUS   He dumped me
I threw my plate against the wall
I'm ugly, I'm fat
And I hate myself

Martin's Story (2)

MARTIN is lying asleep in bed.
He wakes up.

MARTIN   Today's the day!
I can feel it

He ticks off the day on the chalkboard.

Thirty-four days

He goes to the window and looks out.

Baltic!

He goes through his morning routines.

Morning Mr Mirror
You look happier today
Mr Sink, how are you?
Morning Mr Fridge
Can I have a can of Coke please?
No, sugar is bad for you
Make it a Diet Coke
No, Diet Coke gives you cancer
I'll have a fruit juice
Drinking fruit juice is bad for your digestive system
I'll have milk
No, milk is bad for you too
I'll drink water
Water out of the tap is bad for you
I'll drink a bottled water
Which one?
Evian…
Evian?
Marie!

Sorry Mr Fridge
I don't need you this morning

He rushes to the computer.
He starts to type.

'Dear Marie
Sorry I couldn't make it last night
I was on my way when I met two friends of mine'

He looks briefly at sink and fridge.

'In George Square, who told me my Auntie Senga
Who's not really my auntie but I call her that
Was seriously ill in hospital and
I had to visit her right away'

Yawn.

'There will be another…'

Yawn.

'…time when we can…'

Yawn.

'…we can meet…'

He falls asleep at computer.

Music. Dream sequence. No 'dialogue'.
He wakes up, boldly opens the seven bolts and walks out past the bus stop into the city for his rendezvous with Marie. She is there, they shake hands and she is delighted with his physical appearance and his conversation. They go for a drink in a nice city bar where the barman welcomes **MARTIN** *as a friend. He downs a pint, she a glass of wine. She sees the time and they go to the cinema together and watch a film. They touch hands for a moment and then Marie slips out of* **MARTIN**'s *dream.*
Music stops.

MARTIN *wakes up at his computer.*
He continues typing to Marie.

'I think today would be a nice opportunity for us to meet. Yours sincerely…'

He clicks 'send'.
He looks over at the door.
He gets up and gets back into his bed.

Playground Risk for Children in Peacetime (2)

CHORUS Make sure spaces that could trap and strangle children, such as openings in guard rails or between ladder rungs, measure less than three point five inches or more than nine inches. Check for dangerous hardware, like open S hooks or protruding bolt ends. Look out for tripping hazards, like steps, trees and rocks. Be on constant alert and the children can have safe fun.

Tips for Teams

CHORUS AVOID
Gangs
Bullies

Bad teachers
Paedophiles
Strangers
Muggers
Internet predators
Pornographers
Drivers
Dealers
Smokers
Drinkers
Lenders
Examiners

No Underachievement
No Failure
No Truant
No Depression
No Junk food
No Crash diet
No Binge drinking
No Borrowing
No Nicking
No Cheating
No Lateness
No Infection
No Addiction
No Self-harm
No Grossness
No Violence

No
Disrespect

Go
Shopping

Annmarie's Story (2)

Solo with movement.

ANNMARIE I never do things by halves.
When I danced I danced from the minute I got there
Until they turned off the music and put on the lights.
I never stopped.

I lost myself completely when I danced
I was just so happy
I used to wake up the next morning aching all over.

When I started drinking I was the same
I drank more and I drank longer than anyone else
I hated the taste I hated wine whisky beer the whole lot –
I just had coke with vodka in it, even that made me gag.
Then I got a taste for Baileys.
I liked a peach schnapps and lemonade first time I had one.
After that white wine was easy
You can acquire a taste for anything if put your mind to it.
I kept at it.
Soon, I drank anything
I'd drink a bottle of white spirit
If you told me it would make me drunk fast.
I just wanted it to work on me as quickly as possible,
So I didn't have to think about what I was doing
Just lose myself, have a real laugh, whatever –
Enjoy the rush that comes as the alcohol
Bites into your system

It cost quite a lot but I always had a job
I was a Saturday girl in Greggs
And I had a paper round.
I always had a bank account
Very organized in that way
And if I got short, I'd sell a few CDs, accessories, whatever
   – just stuff.
I'd walk to school and save my bus fare
I'd save my lunch money and have a packet of crisps
Little things really
But it left you more money for a really big night out
Anyway, we'd save by getting pissed at home before we left,
Then taking a bottle in with us and just buying mixers.

I spent more on make-up and clothes than before.
I had to. With dancing I *lost* weight.
Drinking has the opposite effect, in my case.
After a bit, I lived a double life
'Cause I didn't always get home after one of those nights.
I told my parents I was at my friend's in Paisley

When in fact – once or twice –
I couldn't actually remember where I'd ended up.
Once I talked to my mum for twenty minutes and I didn't
  even know where I was!
Most of the time me and the girls looked after each other
But there were times none of us could look after ourselves
Let alone each other…
There were some great nights that are a complete blank.
You tell me what I did
I'll believe you.
It was like that.
Crazy fun.

ANNMARIE collapses into the arms of those around her.

One night, Lisa, a pal of mine, got so wasted
She ended up in Casualty in Glasgow General.
She didn't know what she'd been drinking –
She thought someone had spiked her drink.
I had to sit there with her for a whole Saturday night and
  Sunday.
Then she calmed down and they let her go.
I told my mum I was at Lisa's and Lisa told her mum she
  was at mine.
The people who were coming in all through the night looked
  so terrible,
They were pissed and full of cursing and abuse,
Most of them cut up through fights or accidents,
So much blood.

Sometime in the night Lisa stopped crying and fell asleep
I went to the ladies' –
I saw myself in the mirror under the hospital lights
I was so shocked at what I saw.
I looked a complete wreck.
I wanted to spit at the face looking back at me.

I knew what I wanted to do in that moment.
I wanted to quit
I didn't want to be here ever again
I don't know who I was trying to please getting pissed all the
  time
I just knew I was totally unhappy doing this

I couldn't understand why I'd stopped dancing.
I'd given up myself
And I'd become someone else.
But was this new person me?
Why was I here, spending a weekend with the living dead?
I went back to Lisa who was crying
She was about to be sick yet again…
That's why I'm here – of course!
I helped her into the ladies'.

Voices (7)

BOYS   Death makes you feel alive

If I do this
If I do it
If I survive
Then I get something back

I'm not scared of Death but
Even if I was
I'd still make Death more scared of me
Than I am of him

I'll look him in the eyes
I'll look him in the sockets
I'll stare him out
I'll scare the shit out of him

If he looks away first,
Then I'll feel twice as alive
As I do now

I'm not scared of Death

Michelle's Story (2)

Solo with movement.

MICHELLE   One place we hung out at was called 'The Warehouse'.
It was a semi-ruined old bomb factory hidden just off the
    motorway…
Sometimes we flocked there, thirty to forty of us, with our
    carry-outs.
Even though I was small I was always the one who went into
    the offy.

I had the voice and the confidence.

We'd get there and it was a crazy party of thirteen, fourteen
 and fifteen year-olds
All falling off walls and running through tunnels and
 screaming our heads off.
I remember the girls nicking one boy's clothes
And him running home with *nothing on*.
It was wet and cold and he had a long way to go.
It was so funny to us all in the state we were in.
We just didn't think, the madder it got the better.
Everything went on there.
Everything.

One night, when I was fourteen years old,
I walked about a mile in the dark alone
To meet Lorraine and the others there.
There were rumours that The Warehouse was unsafe,
There were unexploded bombs.
That night we went right *inside* the building
Where walls and stairwells had collapsed into heaps of brick
 and rubble.
We jumped all over them pissed out of our minds –
I remember jumping off a two-storey roof and rolling down a
 hill.

I came to a stop, still laughing my head off and
Lorraine was there, really scowling, standing very still.
'You drank my cider.'
'No I didn't,' I said, 'I bought my own.'
'Yeah – and then you drank mine.'
'No – '
'Then how come you're pissed and I'm sober?'
She turned on me, like *that*.
This time she really hurt me and there was no way I could
 stand up to her.
No one helped me.
The boys just stood there and gawked.
I trusted her like I'd always trusted friends.
But I wasn't her friend.
She and her friends never really liked me.
Even after eighteen months.

This is what I didn't understand.
I was her hostage.
She was just waiting for her moment.

I walked back home and I never felt so low in my life.
I went from drunk to sober in a moment,
I was bruised from Lorraine's kicking
but – more – I was hurt that she'd turned against me.
My parents were away at a conference so I got no questions.
I cleaned up and went to bed.
I didn't get up for the whole weekend,
I didn't open the curtains.

Everything was tangled up together and
I couldn't unknot it in my mind – what I did,
What Lorraine did to me,
What I'd done to others.

A cloud entered my room
Even though the curtains were closed.
It started as a small ball of mist
In the middle of the ceiling and
It grew until it covered the ceiling and
Started to fill my room.
It got to my bed and
So I lay on the floor and
Then it got to the floor and
It covered me.

I crawled under the bed.
It was dark and I felt safer.
But I started shaking and I couldn't stop.
It was like having vertigo after you've jumped.

My parents came home on Sunday night and
Asked me why I'd never answered my phone.
I said I'd heard it ringing
But I couldn't get up.
That was true.
My dad wasn't bothered
Because he had a lot of important calls to make.
My mum asked a lot of questions.
I talked a lot and I told her nothing.

They both thought I'd just had too much to drink.
I had – but that was just a fraction of what I'd been doing.

They went back to work on Monday.
Somehow I pulled myself together and dragged myself to
  school.

Back at school I didn't really know who I was anymore.
My old friends wouldn't speak to me and Lorraine and her
  pals just laughed. They made a very cruel joke that I just
  want to forget.
Lorraine said I could have a fight any time I liked.

Voices (8)

GIRLS   My body
        Fat thin tall small little big
        My body
        Straight square round long short wide
        My body
        I want to be smaller thinner lighter darker sharper flatter
          bigger stronger
        My body
        I'm stuck inside
        My body
        I'm am no less and no more than the sum of the parts that
          make up
        My body
        I'm turning changing growing spreading and it's still
        My body
        I'm sexy as hell just look at
        My body
        I'm not, I'm small and fat and I'm not sexy at all just look at
        My body
        I'm six foot tall, I'm a woman, my body arrived in the night, I
          frighten myself when I look in the bathroom mirror, I'm new
          to
        My body
        Don't touch
        My body
        Please touch
        My body

It's just
My body
I'll do just what I like with
My body

Flaunt it
Hate it
Hide it
Change it

Flay it
Chance it
Trash it
Waste it

Leave it
Fake it
Hurt it
Treat it

Watch it
Touch it
Spoil it
Love it

Sometimes whatever I do
I feel kind of dead
And no one cares what I say or what I do
I feel like I'm just floating in nothing
I wish I could leave
My body

Ed's Story (2)

ED   My parents had rigid expectations
Of who I was meant to be,
Where I belonged,
How I should behave,
What I was going to do with my life and what I wasn't.
My mum's quite religious, my dad's not.
He's just very fixed in his way of thinking.
After his assault on me,
I was really shocked because though I had fights with my
    brothers,

My dad had never actually hit me before.

I didn't know who I was anymore.

I couldn't stay in my home any longer.

If I ever belonged there, I didn't anymore.

I packed a rucksack and climbed out my bedroom window at
 ten o'clock

That was when I usually came home.

I don't why I did that,

I could have walked out the front door.

No one would have stopped me.

They wanted me to go!

I didn't know where I was going.

I couldn't believe what I was doing.

This was for me, for my life.

I hitched a lift south on the London Road with a boy about
 my age.

He didn't say much.

He was driving a big car so fast I was totally petrified.

At Gretna Green he said, 'This as far south as I go.'

He dumped me and did a U-turn.

I'm sure he'd stolen it and was just having a ride in a big
 machine.

It was 2 AM and it was raining.

The train station had signs pointing in two directions.

One said Scotland and the other said England.

I lay down in a waiting room and went to sleep.

DANCE.

Voices (9)

CHORUS   Shout I

Big I not little me

Write my own script

I am potent

Omnipotent

I do my deed

I flash my arse

I cross the ice

I steal the bike

I don't knock
I break and enter
I like the risk

Risk never stops
We take a risk –
We succeed,
We fail.
Whatever the outcome,
There is another risk to take,
Another choice to make.
Risk makes risk.

Martin's Story (3)

MARTIN is lying asleep in bed.
He wakes up.

MARTIN Today's the – forget it!

He ticks off the day on the chalkboard.

Thirty-five days

He chucks away the chalk.
He goes to the window and looks out.

Baltic!

He goes through his morning routines.

(*To mirror.*) Who you looking at?
Told yer I'm not talking to you!

(*To sink.*) Shut it Mr Sink, I'll turn the tap on whenever I want

(*To fridge.*) Shut it Frostie, you got nothing I can eat or drink
   anymore

(*To computer.*) And as for you
My best pal
My oldest friend
My special mate
You are the reason for all of this stuff
You are a lead weight around my neck
If it wasn't for you I would have done this long ago

He puts on his jacket.

Oh it's disgusting is it?
It's well out of date?
People will laugh?
Will they?
I don't care
I'm going
You cannot stop me
And save your tears
I know you're really a crocodile

He opens the seven bolts and faces the open door.
He walks into the doorway and stops.
He is ready to walk.
Will he do so?

Annmarie's Story (3)

ANNMARIE   (*Dancing.*) All I know is
It's a risk for me to be me

I want to do what is right for me
Not what anyone tells me

I want to dance again
But next Friday
What'll I do?
When my friends go out for a drink…
Will I dare to be me?

CHORUS *join* **ANNMARIE** *dancing.*

Michelle's Story (3)

MICHELLE   Lorraine had a baby
I did my highers
We lost touch
I learnt a lot from her.
I'll never be bullied again.

Movement only: **MICHELLE** *executes a sequence of Tae Kwon Do moves with sustained power.*

DANCE / MUSIC.

Ed's Story (3)

ED   I went on to London but I only stayed a week.
I never knew how much I loved my own city.
I saw that my family was the problem,
Not Glasgow.
So I moved into a friend's house
And I trained to be a librarian.
Her family used to go walking at the weekends in the
  Campsies
Not far outside the city.
Proper walks in boots and anoraks with sandwiches in your
  bag.
Sometimes I went with them.
I liked it.
That's the first time I saw the human kites –
Paragliders.

CHORUS paraglide to divine pop music.

Paul's Story (2)

PAUL I've moved on.
I do a job
Just like anyone else.
I sleep at night now.
I'm not listening for the door.
I earn a wage
And not a gold piece anymore.
It's enough.
Not easy though
With only a tenner in your pocket
At eight o'clock on a Friday night.
I had to find something new.
Fast.
Something to give me that power
I always wanted –
Free running, free runner, freedom…
To me, they're the one and the same.
You'll never catch me.
I go training most nights.
Great guys doing it, made some friends.

I'm losing my fear of heights.
Crime taught me to focus.

Parkour / Free Running Section

PAUL & COMPANY For the citizens of Glasgow
The normal way to cross the city
Is horizontal.
By road or rail.
By squares and corners
Forwards, backwards,
Left, right.
Stop bus, station, pavement, car;
The long routes,
Block by block.

For free runners
Glasgow is a vertical city.
There are other routes;
Over fences and trees
Ledges, railings, walls,
Steps, bollards, skylights
From parapet to roof,
Roof to floor,
Roof to roof,
There are no limits
Only obstacles.

Our routes run where it is possible to run
Across round under over above
Flying cars in the future?
The vertical stroller is already here
He walks on air

Free running
Liquid movement
Aerial dancing
Sky tracing
Parkour…

No traffic jams on route
Only obstacles
No stopping

Free running
No limits

Specific moves:

Cat leap
Wallrun
Underbar
Tic toc
Roll
Three-sixty

A roof is the shortest route between two walls

To fly
Your head
Matters more
Than wings

The whole city is my playground

Voices (10)

CHORUS We fight the feeling of emptiness
We throw ourselves into the void.
We take vertigo into freefall

End.